Beauty oils & butters

ELAINE STAVERT

Beauty oils & butters

GUILD OF MASTER CRAFTSMAN PUBLICATIONS

First published in 2010 by
Guild of Master Craftsman Publications Ltd
Castle Place, 166 High Street,
Lewes, East Sussex BN7 1XU

ISBN: 978-1-86108-691-4

Associate Publisher: Jonathan Bailey
Production Manager: Jim Bulley
Managing Editor: Gerrie Purcell
Editor: Beth Wicks
Managing Art Editor: Gilda Pacitti
Designer: Rob Janes

Set in Gill Sans

Colour origination by GMC Reprographics
Printed and bound by Hing Yip Printing Co. Ltd in China

Please note that imperial measurements throughout are
approximate conversions from metric. When following
the instructions, use either the metric or the imperial
measurements, do not mix units. For further information
refer to the table on page 148.

Why we love oils and butters

Oils and butters will soothe and soften.
Apply them daily and bathe with them often.
Nurture your skin with some well-deserved care,
or apply a conditioning treatment to your hair.

With recipes for your baby, granny and father,
a natural product we know you would rather.
By making your own for family and friends,
a luxurious time we know they will spend.

There are ingredients known to make your skin shine
and aromatic scents to help you feel fine.
For a relaxing evening is the aim
after a long hard day, or a tennis game.

Present your friends with a gorgeous potion
to help them de-stress and calm their emotion.
Make a luxurious gift, use your imagination
to blend and scent a unique creation.

But is it fun we hear you utter?
Just try and you'll see why we love oils & butters.

Contents

Introduction and history

We've all had times in our life when our skin or our spirits have needed a boost. By using the precious oils that nature has given us in the seeds and nuts of plants we, like our ancestors, can help to improve the texture and feel of our skin while helping to ease aches, pains and other ailments.

Oils can nourish and protect, lubricate and moisturize, soften and ease. They are also used to carry essential oils or perfume for the purpose of massage, bathing, ointments, salves and soothing balms.

By continuing to use these oils we are taking another step in the long history of bathing, with aromatic oils, perfumes and herbs having been used since time immemorial to anoint, scent and cleanse the body for the purpose of worship, hygiene, good health and spiritual well-being.

Ancient Egyptian oils

Throughout the ancient world, Egypt was famous for the production and export of expensive floral perfumes and fragrances. Plenty of sunshine and a steady supply of water meant many exotic crops thrived, and ancient Egypt quickly emerged as the central area of the western Eurasian cosmetic trade.

Cleanliness, bathing and aromatic oils were highly important to the ancient Egyptians. They were prolific bathers, spending hours on their ablutions, after which they smothered their bodies with perfumed oils to nourish and protect their skin. The hieroglyphics found in ancient Egyptian tombs, the papyrus and perfume bottles buried there, and the writings of the ancient physicians and herbalists Dioscorides and Pliny, provide us with details and recipes of ancient Egyptian perfumes and unguents. These blends of precious oils were often made by priests who were used to blending perfumes for worship and rituals.

Oils for luxury

Scented oils were in use from very early on in Egypt. As early as 2000 BC fragrant resins and unguents were transported on merchant ships from other countries in the Mediterranean, India and other distant places.

The oils would have been moringa, safflower, balanos, linseed, castor, olive or almond. These would have been scented with botanicals such as cinnamon, myrrh, lily, marjoram, juniper, fir or saffron. Gum and resin, such as frankincense and myrrh, were added as fixatives to perfumes, as well as being used for their scent and therapeutic properties. Moringa oil in particular would have been used to adorn the hair and to create cosmetic creams.

To make a perfume in the absence of alcohol, these precious herbs and spices were infused in vegetable oils such as balanos (a native tree with a date-like fruit), moringa (a native desert tree from Thebes), olive, castor, sesame and almond oil or animal fats. Expensive luxury perfumes, such as 'The Egyptian', made from cinnamon and myrrh, 'Metopion', a mix of bitter almonds and galbanum, and 'Susinum', an unguent made from balanos oil infused with lilies, were worn to attract potential lovers and played a large part in romance and love-making. Queen Cleopatra was famously reputed to have used aromatic perfumes in abundance, not just for bathing but also in the seduction of Mark Antony by adorning her ships with garlands of scented flowers and perfumes.

Medicinal uses

Aromatic medicinal oils were also derived from the abundance of available botanicals such as acacia, basil, celery, chamomile, cinnamon, cumin, dill, fir, iris, juniper, lily, marjarom, rose, sage and pine. Some medicines were taken internally, while others were used as a poultice, unguent or inhalation. The famous remedy 'Metopion' was used to ease aching limbs and ulcers. It was made from a blend of mainly imported ingredients: almond, camel grass, sweet flag, galbanum, balsamum seed, cardamom, myrrh, honey and wine.

Another famous traditional Egyptian recipe was 'Kyphi', known to be relaxing, purifying and sleep-inducing. This was drunk as a cleansing herbal beverage to ease ailments such as snake bites, complaints of the liver or lungs, asthma, coughs and chest infections. The base of the recipe was mashed raisins, honey and wine combined with myrrh, other resins, herbs and spices.

Scents for worship

Deep in the innermost room of a temple the deity would be presented and anointed daily with fragrant gifts of oils and incense. The ancient Egyptians believed that if they kept the gods happy with gifts and sacrifices they would be rewarded with good crops, plenty of water and fertility.

Using aromatic incense in worship was considered a way not only of gratifying the gods, but also bringing together a deceased king with other deities who would help guide him towards his eternal life in the cosmos. When a king died his body would be anointed with aromatic oils, not only to remove the odour of death, but also to restore and unite his physical body in the afterlife, making him sweet-smelling and whole again upon meeting the gods.

Basic Techniques

Equipment and materials

You will not need any complicated equipment to make the recipes in this book; in fact, you will probably have most of it in your kitchen already.

Even the raw ingredients are easily obtained from the growing number of mail order 'cosmetic supplies' companies (see suppliers on page 149).

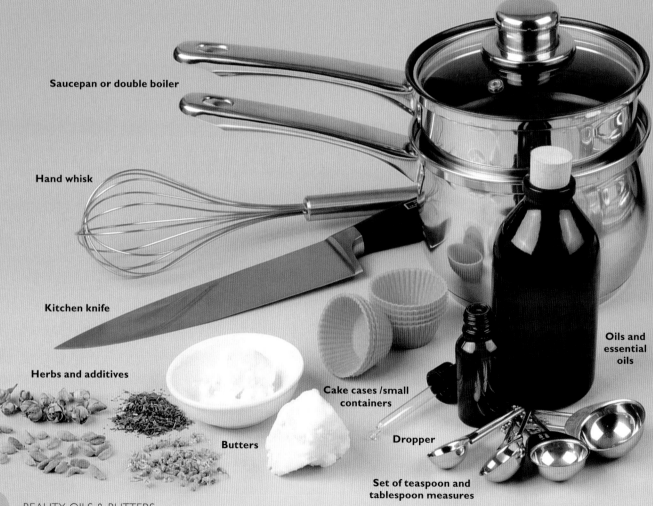

Saucepan or double boiler

Hand whisk

Kitchen knife

Herbs and additives

Butters

Cake cases /small containers

Dropper

Set of teaspoon and tablespoon measures

Oils and essential oils

Weighing scales

Greaseproof or baking paper

Plastic containers

Non-metal
measuring jug

Plastic or metal spoon or spatula

Clean empty bottles or jars

Wax

Bath and body oils

Bath and body oils are extremely easy to make. They are not only a wonderful way to moisturize your body and soften your skin, but they are also used as 'carriers' of essential oils to ensure that these are safe and easy to apply to your skin.

Making bath and body oils

Blend all the oils together with your essential oils or fragrance and pour into bottles. It is best to store the oils in amber or coloured glass bottles somewhere cool and away from daylight in order to preserve the properties of the oils and essential oils.

Basic massage and body oil recipe

8¾oz (250ml) oil mixed with ½ teaspoon (2.5ml) essential oils.

For oils that remain on the skin use up to a maximum of 1% (2 teaspoons or 10ml) of fragrance or essential oil per 35oz (1 litre) of oil. For use on children under the age of seven use a maximum of 0.5% (1 teaspoon or 5ml).

Caution: You should never apply essential oils directly to the skin as this can cause severe skin irritation. Essential oils are therefore always diluted in carrier oils, these literally carry the essential oil to your skin, making application safe and easy.

Macerated oils

Macerated oils are oils that are infused with herbs. The herb's essential oils are imparted into a vegetable oil, providing the therapeutic properties and sometimes the colour of the herb. Some common and useful macerated oils are calendula (marigold), borage, comfrey, arnica and St John's Wort.

Making macerated oils

It is easy to make your own macerated oils.

1 Place dried herbs or flowers in a clean jar with a tight-fitting lid. Add enough oil, such as sweet almond, apricot, olive, sunflower or jojoba, to cover the herbs approximately 1½ times, then leave for 6–8 weeks, remembering to shake the jar daily.

2 To speed up the process you can heat the mixture over a very gentle heat. Be careful not to let the oil get too hot as this will destroy the properties of the plant. Hot oil on a stove can also be a fire risk.

3 Finally, strain then pour the macerated oil into clean dark glass bottles. Label these clearly. The oil will keep for several months, or longer if you use jojoba oil.

Basic bath oil recipe

8¾oz (250ml) oil mixed with ½–1 teaspoon (2.5–5ml) essential oils.

For bath oils add 1–2% (2–4 teaspoons or 10–20ml) of fragrance or essential oil per 35oz (1 litre) of oil. Do not add more than 3% (2 tablespoons or 30ml) as it may irritate your skin. Use only 0.5% (1 teaspoon or 5ml) for children under the age of seven.

Body butters

A body butter is a solid vegetable butter that is combined with a liquid oil, such as olive or sweet almond, to make a soft mixture. Body butters are rich, emollient and easily applied to your skin. If you wish to cut down on the oiliness of your butter you can add a little cornflour (cornstarch).

Basic body butter recipe

4oz (120g) vegetable butter

3oz (80g) liquid oil, such as sweet almond, grapeseed or olive

40 drops (2ml) essential oil (or essential oil blend) or fragrance oil

½ teaspoon (2.5ml) vitamin E oil (optional)

1–2 teaspoons (5–10ml) pearlescent mica to add a shimmering glow (optional)

1–2 tablespoons (15–30ml) herbs or alkanet (optional)

To 35oz (1kg) of body butter mixture we recommend adding a maximum of 1% (2 teaspoons or 10ml) of fragrance or essential oil. For children under the age of seven a maximum of 0.5% (10 drops) should be used.

Note: Butters such as avocado or aloe can be very soft, so either reduce the amount of liquid oil in the recipe or combine them with a harder butter such as cocoa or shea butter.

Making a body butter

1　Gently melt the butter, oil and any herbs, such as alkanet (a natural pink colourant), in a double saucepan or a saucepan placed over another pan of simmering water. It is possible to melt the butter directly on the heat in a heavy-based pan, but you will need to keep a careful eye on it in case the butter gets too hot and the precious vitamins are destroyed.

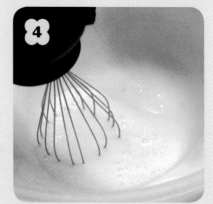

2   Remove from the heat and add the oil to the melted butter.

3   Transfer the mixture to a bowl and place it in a basin of iced water, then add the essential oils.

4   Whip the mixture with a hand whisk. It will gradually turn from a golden colour to a light cream.

5   Add the mica, if using. Then keep whisking until the texture resembles whipped cream.

6   Spoon into containers and leave to set for 24 hours.

Soaps

The main component of vegetable glycerine soap base is vegetable oil to which butters and essential oils are added. Select an oil or butter that suits your skin type or one that will provide the therapeutic properties you require.

A very quick, safe and easy way to make your own soap is to use a ready-made 'melt and pour' vegetable glycerine soap base, which is widely available (see the suppliers list on page 149). Use a SLS-free, natural, or organic soap base as they do not contain harsh surfactants, which can dry out your skin. Simply melt down the base, add your choice of herbs, scent and colour, pour into containers and leave to set.

Finding moulds

Many household objects and packaging make ideal soap moulds. Any plastic container can be used, as long as it has flexible sides to make removing the soap easier. If you are using thin plastic food packaging, make sure the melted soap base is not too hot as it may melt or warp the mould.

Ready-made soap moulds are also widely available. These usually have several moulds on one sheet and are available in a huge range of designs including shells, stars and animals. Moulds designed for chocolate-making are also suitable and are especially good for making small guest soaps.

Basic soap recipe

35oz (1kg) organic (natural or SLS-free) vegetable glycerine soap base
1 tablespoon (15ml) herbs (do not use flower petals, except calendula, as they will go brown)
1 tablespoon (15ml) melted butter or oil (avocado, rose hip etc)
Up to 1 teaspoon (5ml) liquid colour
4 teaspoons (20ml) essential oil or fragrance oil

Making a soap

1 First, calculate how much soap base to use. Fill your chosen mould with water, then pour into a measuring jug. The amount of water in the jug will be the amount of melted soap you need: 32oz (1 litre) = approximately 2¼lbs (1kg).

2 On a chopping board cut the soap base into 1–2in (25–50mm) chunks using a kitchen knife. Place the chunks in a large non-metal measuring jug or heavy-based saucepan.

3 To melt the soap place the measuring jug in a microwave and heat on full power. Start with 20 seconds and continue in 10-second bursts until the base is melted, stirring between bursts. Stirring should disperse small chunks of soap without further heating.

Alternatively, melt the soap base on top of the stove in a heavy-based saucepan or double boiler. Heat gently, stirring, until the soap is almost melted, then turn off the heat and stir until the rest of the soap melts.

Whichever method you chose, melt the base gently until it becomes liquid. Do not overheat as it may burn and become thick, cloudy or caramel coloured. It may also warp thin moulds. Avoid getting any hot soap on your skin.

Adding extra ingredients

Once the base has melted you can then add a variety of different ingredients to give your soap colour, texture or fragrance. These may be in the form of powders, liquids, waxes, oils or dried or fresh herbs. Make sure you only use skin-safe ingredients, never ones intended for pot pourri or candle-making, and mix in very thoroughly to distribute evenly. See the basic soap recipe on page 20 for some suitable additives and recommended quantities.

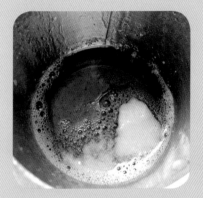

Preparing the additives

Mix any powdered ingredients with a little water before adding to the soap base, to prevent clumping. Gently melt additives such as beeswax, hard oils or butters in a double saucepan or the microwave, taking care not to overheat them. Mix thoroughly to ensure even distribution before adding to the soap base.

Fragrance

Soaps may be scented with essential oils or synthetic fragrance oils. The recommended quantity is 2–4 teaspoons (10–20ml) of fragrance or essential oil to every kilo of soap base, or 1–2% of weight. Do not add more than 3% as this may irritate the skin or turn the soap cloudy. Do not add colourings before the fragrance stage as some scents are naturally coloured and may colour your soap base slightly.

Colour

The easiest way to add colour is using cosmetic-grade water-based liquid colour added, drop-by-drop. Stir in the colour thoroughly to ensure even distribution. Soap colours are often very concentrated and just half a drop may be all that is needed. Remember that the strength or dilution of liquid colour may vary depending on the supplier.

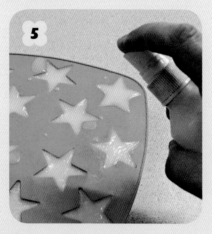

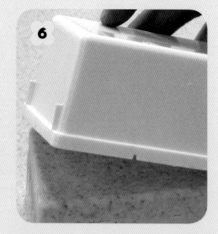

4 When the melted soap base contains all the extra ingredients you want to include (see box on page 22) pour into your chosen mould.

5 After pouring, small bubbles may appear on the surface of the soap, which will set and spoil its appearance. Spritz or spray the bubbles with surgical spirit or alcohol to make them disappear. If you do not have any surgical spirit to hand, smooth over the bubbles using the back of a spoon. Leave to set for at least 24 hours.

6 When the soap has set, gently pull the sides of the mould away from the soap. Turn the block upside-down and gently press the mould until the soap pops out.

7 Cut your soap into bars using either a kitchen knife, a soap cutter or a crinkle-edged potato chip cutter.

Notes: Vegetable glycerine soaps will sweat if left unwrapped, so wrap your soap in plastic food wrap or cellophane.

The soaps are best used within 6–12 months. Make sure that they are not left in direct light as any colour will fade very quickly, particularly if you have used powdered herbs as a colourant.

Balms

A balm is a liquid oil, such as olive or sweet almond oil, which is combined with melted butter and wax in order to harden the mixture. Balms can be used on lips and on other parts of the body as salves and soothing ointments.

Beeswax has been used for the balm recipes in this book. Vegan alternatives to beeswax include olive, almond, candelilla, carnauba, jojoba, hemp and rice bran wax. Macerated oils, essential oils and flavour oils can all be added to the balms.

Basic balm recipe

1½oz (45g) oil such as olive or sweet almond (weighed)
½oz (15g) beeswax
½oz (15g) shea or cocoa butter
15 drops essential oil (or cosmetic flavour oil for lip balms)
½ teaspoon (2.5ml) vitamin E oil (optional)
1–2 teaspoons herbs or alkanet (optional)

Notes: You may wish to add macerated or other precious oils for their therapeutic benefit. Simply deduct the amount used from the main oil amount. For example, if you use ½oz (15g) argan oil (weighed), the remaining liquid oil content should be reduced to 1oz (30g) olive oil.

If you are making a lip balm you could use a cosmetic-grade flavour oil instead of an essential oil that could be ingested. The amount of flavour oil or essential oil added to your balms should be no more than 1%. For example, 3½oz (100g) of balm should have no more than 20 drops (1ml) added to the mixture. For children under the age of seven a maximum of 0.5% (10 drops) should be used.

Making a balm

1 Gently melt the beeswax, oil, butter and vitamin E, together with any herbs, in a double saucepan or in a saucepan set over another pan of simmering water.

2 If you are using alkanet to colour your balm either pink or red you will see the colour of the balm change as the oils melt.

3 Remove from the heat and add the essential oils or flavour oils.

4 If using alkanet as a colourant, strain the herb from the balm.

5 Leave the balm to cool for a few minutes, then pour into little tins or pots. Leave the balms to set for 24 hours.

Note: If you pour the balm out when it is still too hot, your finished balm will have a dip in the middle. To avoid this keep some balm back, reheat it and pour another thin layer on top when the balm is set enough to hold another layer. Alternatively, wait until the balm is fully set, then heat the top with a hair dryer which will briefly melt and even out the surface.

Bath melts

A bath melt is a mixture of melted hard butter, such as cocoa butter, and a liquid oil, such as sweet almond oil, which is left to set into shapes. When added to a warm bath, it will melt and disperse to leave your skin soft and silky.

Basic bath melt recipe

7oz (200g) cocoa butter

3½oz (100g) oil (weighed)

1 teaspoon (5ml) essential oil or fragrance oil

½ teaspoon (2.5ml) vitamin E oil (optional)

½ teaspoon (2.5ml) ultramarine pink powder
mixed with a little oil (optional)

Notes: Bath melts can be coloured with ultramarine powders or lakes, although these should be used very sparingly as you could easily colour yourself and your bath. Mix the colourant with a little liquid oil in order to blend the mixture well and to avoid clumps. Alternatively, use natural herbs as colourants, such as alkanet root (pink) or annatto seeds (yellow/orange). Melt the herbs with the butter and sieve them out before pouring into moulds.

You can also add fragrance to the bath melts. To 35oz (1kg) of bath melt mixture we recommend adding 1–2% (2–4 teaspoons or 10–20ml) of fragrance or essential oil. Do not add more than 3% (2 tablespoons or 30ml) as it may irritate the skin.

In warm weather, keep bath melts in a refrigerator so they do not melt. Clearly mark them 'NOT TO EAT'.

Making bath melts

1   Melt the cocoa butter in a double boiler. Add the liquid oil and any colour mixed with oil (if appropriate). Remove from the heat and add the essential oils.

2   Pour your mixture into the moulds (see below).

3   Leave to set overnight – placing them in a refrigerator will help with unmoulding.

Note: Good moulds to use for bath melts include ice cube moulds or very tiny silicone petit four cases. Regular cupcake tins will create too large bath melts, which will make the bath much too oily; if you want to use them, fill them ¼ to ⅓ full.

Bath truffles

Bath truffles are a mix between bath bombs and melts, gently fizzing as they hit the water, while the butter slowly melts and smooths. They can be decorated with petals, herbs, glitter or mica and will leave the skin refreshed and moisturized.

Basic bath truffle recipe

4½oz (125g) bicarbonate of soda (baking soda)
1¾oz (50g) citric acid
¾oz (25g) cornflour (cornstarch)
1¾oz (50g) cocoa butter
1 teaspoon (5ml) essential oil or fragrance oil
½ teaspoon (2.5ml) vitamin E (optional)
A handful of petals or herbs for decoration

Notes: You can add fragrance to your bath truffles. To 35oz (1kg) of bath truffle mixture we recommend adding 1–2% (2–4 teaspoons or 10–20ml) of fragrance or essential oil. Do not exceed 3% (2 tablespoons or 30ml) as it may irritate your skin.

Add decorations, such as sprinkles, herbs, petals or cocoa powder, to the rolled truffle shapes to make them look even prettier.

Making bath truffles

1 Melt the cocoa butter and vitamin E, if using. Leave to cool for a while, then add the essential oil.

2 Sieve the bicarbonate soda and cornflour, before adding the citric acid. Add the cooled, but still runny oil mixture and stir well.

3 Keep stirring until the mixture is thick enough to hold its shape. Depending on the temperature of the cocoa butter you may need to wait for up to 30 minutes. Keep checking and stirring the mixture during this time as you do not want it to set.

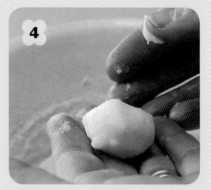

4 Working quickly, take some of the mixture in your hands and shape it into a ball.

5 Roll the ball in the decorations you are using and squeeze these into the ball. Depending on the consistency of the mixture you may need to press these in very firmly.

6 Reshape into a small round ball and place on greaseproof paper.

7 After several hours the balls will harden and become very firm. Leave to set for 24 hours.

Bath bombs

Bath bombs are shapes made from citric acid and bicarbonate of soda that set when water is added. In the bath they fizz and disperse the essential oils and other additives in the water. Bicarbonate of soda softens your skin while the therapeutic properties of the oils do their wonderful work on your body.

Finding moulds

Any small plastic container can be used as a mould for bath bombs, including yoghurt or pudding pots, ice cube trays, tennis balls cut in half, chocolate-making moulds or specific bath bomb or soap moulds (see the suppliers list on page 149). You may wish to place petals or a rose bud in the bottom of the mould for decoration before filling.

Basic bath bomb recipe

10½oz (300g) granulated citric acid
21oz (600g) bicarbonate of soda (baking soda)
1 teaspoon (5ml) liquid colour or powdered ultramarine
1 tablespoon (15ml) essential oil or fragrance oil
1 tablespoon (15ml) oil or melted butter
1 tablespoon (15ml) herbs or petals
A little water to bind the mixture

Notes: You can add colour, texture and fragrance to the bath bombs. To 35oz (1kg) of bath bomb mixture we recommend adding up to 1–2 tablespoons (15–30ml) of oil, melted butter, herbs, petals and glitter, in addition to 1–2% (2–4 teaspoons or 10–20ml) of fragrance or essential oil. Do not add more than 3% (2 tablespoons or 30ml) as it may irritate your skin.

The easiest way to colour bath bombs is by using cosmetic-grade, water-based liquid colour or powdered ultramarines. Use a maximum of ¼ teaspoon (1.25ml) of liquid or powdered colour. If you exceed this you could colour yourself and your bath. When set, the bath bombs should be pastel shades.

Making bath bombs

1 Measure the citric acid into a bowl, then sieve the bicarbonate of soda on top.

2 Make a well with your fingers and add any dry ingredients, herbs, glitter and so on. Add your colour and fragrance followed by any melted butters or oil. The mixture may fizz when you add liquid. This is quite normal; just cover the fizzing liquid with some dry ingredients.

3 Mix all the ingredients together with your hands, making sure that all the colour and fragrance is thoroughly mixed in. To distribute any clumps of colour, rub the mixture between the palms of your hands.

4 Next, spray the mixture several times before mixing it with your hands. You can use a spray bottle or simply dampen your hands under a tap and sprinkle a little water into the mixture from your finger tips. When the water reacts with the other ingredients, the mixture will become icy cold and heavy to the touch. Squeeze the mixture together with your hands before adding more water.

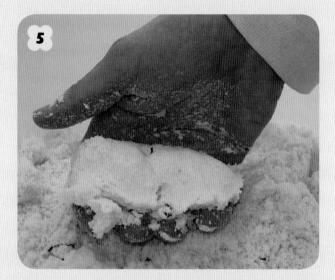

5 The mixture should resemble damp sand and should hold together when squeezed in your fist. If it is dry and crumbly, your bath bomb will not hold together. If this happens, simply add some more water. Add the water a little at a time to avoid adding too much liquid. If the mixture is too wet, when you turn it out it can 'grow' and change shape.

6 When you are happy with the mixture, take a handful and press it into your mould fairly quickly so that it does not dry out.

7 Brush away excess mixture, then with a swift motion firmly place the mould onto a kitchen surface or greaseproof paper. Gently lift the mould away and leave to set for 24 hours.

Perfume and fragrance

Blending essential oils to create a therapeutic fragrance for use in the bath products does not have to be complicated. You can create your own unique blended scents using just a few ingredients, if you follow some basic principles.

The sense of smell

Evolution has given all living organisms the essential survival tools or enzymes that bind to certain smells (odour molecules) to trigger a reaction or emotion. Odours can alert us to danger such as a fire or gas leak, or food that has gone off and may poison us. Young mammals need their olfactory sense to detect their mother's milk for feeding. Some scientists now believe that the process of selecting a partner or mate may unknowingly involve our sense of smell via aromatic chemicals called pheromones.

Humans have approximately 1,000 different kinds of olfactory receptors and can remember up to 10,000 different odours. When we breathe in odorous molecules, they travel up the nose, past olfactory receptor cells, where electrical signals are sent to the brain by nerve processes. A particular smell can instantly trigger very distinctive memories and associations from the past: a childhood trip, a relative, a place of worship, home or other memories, either pleasant or unpleasant.

The human sense of smell (olfaction) has gradually become weaker during evolution; we no longer need to negotiate our environment by our sense of smell as other animals do, or smell the scent of our enemy. Next time you look at a dog's nose twitching, you will know that his olfactory epithelium is around 40 times larger than yours, making his sense of smell up to several million times more powerful.

What is perfume?

The word perfume (parfum) stems from the Latin words *per* meaning 'through', and *fumum* meaning 'smoke'. Early perfumes were produced by burning materials such as wood, gums and resins to give a fragrant smoke (incense), which is still used in places of worship and for meditation today.

A perfume is a blend of fragrant essences and oils obtained from flowers, grasses, resin, bark, gum, fruit, animals and aroma chemicals, dissolved in an alcohol or oil base. Different amounts of these oils are mixed with varying grades of alcohol and water to produce certain strengths, such as toilet water, eau de cologne, eau de toilette and, the strongest and most expensive, eau de parfum and perfume. Perfumes are also used to scent cleaning products, candles, pot pourri, talc, creams, soaps, cosmetics and bath products.

Commercial perfumiers choose from thousands of natural essential oils and synthetic ingredients known as 'aroma chemicals', which are sourced from all corners of the globe. Used like the colours of an artist's palette, many ingredients may be used in formulations and complicated blends to produce olfactory masterpieces. The process of perfume blending is a highly skilful and complicated one, taking years of experience and training to perfect, and requires a particular 'nose' for the job. Just one drop of a precious ingredient added, and left to blend for several days with its counterparts, can literally make the difference between an ordinary and outstanding perfume.

Perfume classifications

Aldehydic A family of aroma chemicals known as aldehydes.

Chypre (meaning 'cypress') Warm and woody with herbaceous, citrus, floral and animalistic notes. Oakmoss, amber, ambergris, patchouli, bergamot and rose.

Citrus Bergamot, lemon, lime, mandarin, orange and petitgrain.

Floral Geranium, jasmine, neroli, rose, ylang ylang and lavender.

Fougère (meaning 'fern') Oakmoss, lavender, coumarin, herbaceous and woody. Mainly men's fragrances.

Gourmand A modern classification of scents resembling food flavours with edible qualities. Notes of vanilla, chocolate and tonka bean.

Green Light and fresh, with ingredients such as galbanum, estragon, violet leaf and helional.

Oceanic A modern classification with clean, crisp aromas.

Oriental Vanilla, florals and woody with animal scents, camphoraceous oils and resins.

Woods Woody scents, sandalwood, cedar and patchouli.

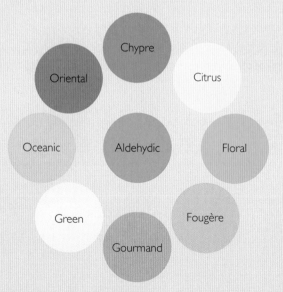

Creating your own blends

The perfume industry uses mostly aroma chemicals in their complex formulas, with essential oils being used only in small amounts to enhance the perfume. There are therefore little, or no therapeutic effects in most perfumes or fragrance oils. The instructions that follow will show you how to create your own essential oil blends which, using aromatherapy, may have therapeutic benefits.

You will, however, not be able to create your own fragrance oil using essential oils. If you wish to have a flavour such as chocolate, apple, passionfruit, blueberry muffin, pina colada, mango, sea breeze etc., you will need to purchase a ready-made fragrance oil that has been produced with aroma chemicals (see suppliers list on page 149).

You could, of course, mix fragrance oils together to create different scents. For instance you could purchase a coconut fragrance oil and a pineapple fragrance oil and blend them together to make your own 'pina colada' fragrance. Or you could blend together a few fruity fragrances to create your own 'fruit salad' fragrance oil. As mentioned before, these fragrance oils will not have any therapeutic benefits; they are purely for fun and aroma pleasure.

Important note

Please note that the instructions here are to enable you to create your own scent for use in cosmetics and bath products. These are NOT perfumes or fragrances to spray on the body, and, as with all essential oils, should NEVER be used neat on the body or in the bath.

Get to know your scents

First, become familiar with your essential oils and make sure that you keep notes of your findings, for if you create a stunning fragrance you will want to make sure that you know exactly how it was formulated.

When smelling an essential oil, do not put your nose directly over the top of the oil and vigorously sniff, otherwise you will get the full blast of the molecules up your nose and the scent will remain in the nostrils for some time making it very difficult for you to smell any more odours for some while.

Prepare some strips of paper (coffee filter bags are perfect) with which to blot some of the oil and waft the scent gently to and fro under your nose letting the fragrance lift upwards, and breathe in slowly. You will usually only be able to sample around six scents at a time before you get nose fatigue. If you are smelling the scent directly from the bottle, it is important to note that you will not be getting the full aroma of the scent. To fully appreciate the aroma you should smell a scent from your paper-testing strips as it can smell quite different once out of the bottle.

If your nose becomes overpowered go outside to clear your nasal passages, or wave your hand under your nose to bring in clear air. If you have a cold, or if you smoke, this will impair your sense of smell. Take breaks every so often as sampling essential oils for long periods at a time may cause headaches or nausea. Our notes in the Essential oils section (see pages 64–84) will help you to describe the scents of your oils, but get used to writing down descriptions of the aromas that you experience. Blind-testing yourself is always a useful and fun way of learning.

Top, middle and base notes

A perfume (fragrance) is made up of top, middle and base notes. The **top notes** or 'head' notes are small molecules and are the first ones that you notice when sampling the fragrance. Assertive, bright and initially strong, they stimulate the senses and create the first impression of a fragrance. These volatile fresh, sharp top notes are powerful and intense to begin with, but they are the first notes to disappear in a fragrance.

When the top notes start to disappear, the **middle notes** begin to come through. These generally warm, soft and mellow oils provide the heart and body of your fragrance, rounding it off and giving it complexity. They ease and pave the way for the next level of oils to emerge.

The **base notes** are usually heavy, exotic, intensely sensual and warm, they are generally woody or resinous materials. These strong aromas will be the last scents to be detected, they linger longest and 'fix' the whole blend, preventing the top and middle notes from evaporating too quickly.

A harmonious blend

The aim is to find a good balance of top, middle and base notes. For example, do not overpower a precious jasmine oil with too many pungent spicy balsamic notes; let the 'celebrity' or special oils speak for themselves, and surround them with oils that support and enhance them. This takes practice and skill and also depends on personal preference.

There are, however, no hard and fast rules. You could just use one essential oil, or two oils blended together. You may wish to take just three oils – a top, middle and a base note, see how they blend together, then add other ingredients, or change the amount of drops used. Start off with simple blends, and use only small amounts of of oil, so that you do not make expensive mistakes. Once your confidence has grown, you can use more oils in your blends.

Top notes	Middle notes	Base notes
basil, bergamot, cardamom, clary sage, cypress, eucalyptus, geranium, ginger, grapefruit, juniper, lavender, lemon, lemongrass, lime, mandarin, neroli, orange (sweet), petitgrain, peppermint, pine, rosemary, rose geranium, ylang ylang	black pepper, cardamom, chamomile, clary sage, geranium, ginger, jasmine, juniper, lavender, lemongrass, marjoram, manuka, neroli, palmrosa, petitgrain, pine, rose, rosemary, rose geranium, tea tree, thyme, ylang ylang	cedarwood, frankincense, jasmine, myrrh, patchouli, sandalwood, vetiver

Making a fragrance blend

1 Once you have chosen the essential oils for your scent, write down each ingredient and the amounts, in drops, that you think you will use of each.

2 Using either a bottle with a built-in dropper, or a pipette, drop the first essential oil into a clean glass bottle. Make sure that the drop does not hit the sides of the bottle as the oil will cling to the sides for some time and prevent you from getting the true amounts of oil in the bottom of the bottle.

3 If you are using a pipette, you will need a different one for each essential oil. If the same one is dipped into several oils they will become contaminated with different fragrances and this may ruin your precious essential oils.

Note Make sure that all the drops are the same size: for example, a drop from a pipette held sideways will create a much larger drop than one dropped from holding the pipette straight above the bottle.

4 Develop your fragrance drop by drop; this way if you are unhappy with the end result, you can easily replicate your blend, but omit or replace particular ingredients.

5 Write down each ingredient and the quantities used. Next to each essential oil indicate whether it is a top, middle or base note.

6 Once you have developed your new fragrance, leave it, if possible, for a few days, as the oils will react and blend with each other over this time.

7 To sample, dip a testing strip into your blend to soak up some of the fragrance. Gently wave the testing strip under your nose and breathe in slowly. Leave the testing strip for a few hours, come back and sample again.

8 If you are happy with the fragrance you have created, make a reference in your notes. Use the new blend to create your own bespoke beauty oils and butters.

Important note
Do not forget to label and date your finished blend. Store it in a cool, dark place in a coloured glass bottle, and keep well away from children and pets.

Basic Ingredients

Vegetable oils

Nature has given us an abundance of seeds, nuts and kernels contained in the fruits of plants, providing numerous oils and butters from all over the world, including African shea butter, Asian mango butter, Chinese rice bran oil, American macadamia nut oil and Mediterranean olive oil.

Throughout history, as revealed in ancient Egyptian, Roman and Greek literature, oils extracted from plants (known as vegetable oils) have played an important role. They contain valuable nutrients and are nature's gift for healing and protecting our skin. We continue to use these oils today to nourish, moisturize, soothe, pamper and revitalize our skin.

Our skin is responsible for eliminating waste, yet products containing or derived from petroleum may block the skin's pores making it difficult for toxins to escape. Natural oils work with the body's chemistry. Many of them are high in antioxidants, which help combat the destructive effects of free radicals on the skin caused by pollution, cigarette smoke and the sun's ultra-violet rays. Other oils are known for their therapeutic and skin-renewal benefits, and are used to treat skin conditions such as eczema and psoriasis, aching muscles, or to help reduce scars and wrinkles.

Caution: People with nut allergies should check the suitability of nut oils before using them in recipes.

What are vegetable oils?

Vegetable oils are obtained by pressing, crushing and often refining the seeds, nuts and kernels of plants, and are liquid at room temperature. These parts of the plant's system contain high levels of fatty acids, vitamins and minerals with known antioxidant, anti-inflammatory and moisturizing properties.

The traditional and natural cold-pressing method of oil extraction yields the best quality oil from seeds, leaving it as close as possible to its natural state. Oil is literally squeezed or pressed out, then filtered to remove the sediment or husks. Oils produced in this way have more colour, flavour and smell, and will retain most of their nutrients. Olive oil can be produced by this method; there is a distinct difference in colour between a cold-pressed extra virgin (first pressing) olive oil and a regular olive oil.

More modern methods use high temperatures or petro-chemicals such as hexane, a hydrocarbon with potential carcinogenic properties, to extract the oil. This requires high refining, which results in the removal of many nutrients such as essential fatty acids, chlorophyll and vitamins. Traces of the petrochemicals may also be retained in the oils.

The versatility of vegetable oils is legendary. Apart from their use in the food industry, many oils are widely used to make soaps, skin-care products, cosmetics and candles. Vegetable oils are now also widely used as lubricants, electrical insulators and in the production of biodiesel.

Directory of vegetable oils

Apricots growing

Argan nuts

Avocado oil

Apricot kernel oil

Prunus armeniaca

Pressed from the kernel of the apricot fruit, this light, pale oil is readily absorbed into the skin and makes a good carrier or bath oil. High in essential fatty acids, linoleic and oleic acids, it is beneficial and nourishing to sensitive, dehydrated or mature skin. It is used in skin-care for treating fine lines, delicate and sensitive areas, and is similar to sweet almond or peach oil.

Apricot kernels

Argan oil

Argania spinosa

The nut kernels of the ancient Argan tree, found in the dry, desert conditions of Morocco and North Africa, are hand-pressed to produce this oil. Similar in properties to olive oil, argan oil contains fatty acids and high levels of vitamin E, a powerful antioxidant. The oil has been used by the Berber people for centuries to nourish and protect the skin, and to promote the skin's elasticity, thereby helping to reduce the appearance of scars and wrinkles.

Avocado oil

Persea gratissima

Avocado oil is obtained by pressing the flesh of the fruit. It is easily absorbed into the skin and widely used for sun-damaged or dehydrated skin, eczema and psoriasis. Its emollient properties make it ideal for rejuvenating and softening mature skin. It also makes a good carrier oil.

Avocado

Blackcurrants

Borage

Carrots

Babassu oil

Orbignya oleifera

The fruit of a palm very similar to the coconut palm that grows in the wild of Brazil and South America. It is prized for its moisturizing properties and used to treat dry or inflamed skin. A non-greasy emollient that coats the skin, leaving it silky and smooth. Also effective for oily skin.

Borage

Borago officinalis

From the seeds of the borage plant, also known as 'star flower'. It is the highest form of gamma-linolenic acid, an essential fatty acid required, but not produced, by the body. Traditionally used for skin disorders, including eczema and psoriasis, inflammation, arthritis, and for dry, damaged skin.

Carrot tissue oil

Daucus carota

A golden yellow/orange oil extracted from the flesh of carrots. Packed with vitamins and beta carotene, it is a powerful antioxidant that is extremely useful for cell regeneration as well as for dry, cracked or ageing skin. This strongly coloured oil could also be used to add colour to soaps.

Borage oil

Blackcurrant seed oil

Ribes nigrum

Obtained by the cold pressing of blackcurrant seeds, this vitamin-rich oil, high in gamma-linolenic acid (GLA or omega 6), makes a wonderful addition to face oils, lip balms, hand balms and hair-care products.

Coconut oil (fractionated)

Cocos nucifera

Fractionated coconut is liquid at room temperature. It provides excellent emollient properties, is easily absorbed into the skin and is odourless. It is wonderful for hair-care products and can be added to all other skin-care treatments.

Corn oil

Zea mays

Corn oil is extracted from the germ of the seeds. It is high in vitamin E and essential fatty acids and can be used as a carrier oil and in balms, soaps, bath bombs and bath treats.

Castor oil

Ricinus communis

Obtained from castor beans, castor oil acts as a humectant, drawing moisture to the skin and providing a protective barrier against the environment. Castor oil is also used for sunburn, skin irritation, burns and cuts and is reputed to ease various ailments such as inflammation and muscle pains.

Evening primrose oil

Oenothera biennis

A pale yellow oil produced from the seeds of the evening primrose flower. High in gamma-linolenic acid (GLA or omega 6) it is used to help ease eczema, psoriasis and dry skin. Evening primrose oil is easily absorbed by the skin and used in skin preparations to prevent premature ageing.

Flax

Flax seed (linseed) oil

Linum usitatissimum

A light brown oil high in the natural antioxidants vitamin E and omega 3 providing valuable skin-strengthening and nutritional properties. It is known for its anti-inflammatory properties, which can help reduce the appearance of scarring, stretch marks, redness, acne, eczema and psoriasis.

Grapefruit seed extract

Citrus grandis

Grapefruit seed extract is a thick dark liquid naturally derived from the seeds and pulp of grapefruits. It is used to inhibit the growth of bacteria or mould. The liquid form is also used topically for a variety of skin conditions including acne. Add ¼ teaspoon (1.25ml) to each 35oz (1 litre) melted soap base, bath bomb mixture, balm or butter to help with preservation.

Grapeseed oil

Vitis vinifera seed

A by-product of the wine-making industry, grapeseed oil is made from the seeds of grapes. It is easily absorbed into the skin and is used in the cosmetics industry to support cell membranes, reduce the appearance of stretch marks, and to help repair damaged skin tissue. It makes a good carrier and bath oil.

Grapeseed oil

Hazelnuts growing

Hemp

Jojoba

Hazelnut oil
Corylus americana nut

Hazel trees have long yellow catkins which appear in the spring, the oil is pressed from the hazelnuts. A vitamin-rich oil with excellent emollient properties, containing high levels of thiamine (vitamin B1) and vitamin B6. Hazelnut oil has long been used for the treatment of dry, damaged skin and for filtering the sun's rays and is therefore used in many sun-care products.

Hempseed oil
Cannabis sativa

Extracted from hemp seeds, which are high in important unsaturated fatty acids including palmitoleic, oleic, linoleic and GLA. Hempseed oil is widely used in cosmetics due to the unique balance of its essential fatty acids, which complements the proportions of these acids required by the human body. Hempseed oil also eases inflammation, eczema and psoriasis.

Jojoba oil
Simmondsia chinensis

Jojoba is a native shrub found in the deserts of Arizona, California and Mexico, the oil is a liquid wax obtained from the seeds of the plant. Jojoba oil is similar to our own skin's sebum, produced to protect the skin from becoming dry and to prevent the growth of microorganisms, making it readily absorbed by the skin. It is often used in the cosmetics industry as a fragrance carrier oil and as a moisturizer in skin-care products. Rich in proteins and minerals, jojoba helps soothe eczema, psoriasis, dry and sensitive skin.

Hazelnuts

Kukui nuts

Macadamia nuts

Monoi de Tahiti

Cocos nucifera

The French Polynesians produce Monoi de Tahiti by the process of 'enfleurage', using exotic petals from native tiare flowers gently macerated in refined coconut oil. This ancient method produces an exquisite, floral aroma, making the oil a delightfully fragrant and moisturizing additive. Due to many inferior copies of this oil being sold, Monoi de Tahiti is now a registered 'Appellation d'Origine' and carries a logo assuring its authenticity and quality.

Kukui nut oil

Aleurites moluccana

Used in Hawaii for many years to rejuvenate, moisturise and nourish dry, mature and damaged skin. Kukui nut oil contains vitamins A, C and E and provides antioxidants that help to protect the skin. A non-greasy oil useful for easing sunburn, eczema, psoriasis and sensitive skin.

Macadamia nut oil

Macadamia ternifolia

This oil is produced from the nuts of a native American tree. It contains high levels of palmitoleic acid, a substance similar to the skin's sebum, and is therefore useful for rejuvenating mature, dry and ageing skin, as well as easing stretch marks and burns.

Neem oil

Azadirachta indica

A brown oil with a strong pungent odour. Neem oil originates from India where it has been traditionally used to treat skin disorders such as eczema, psoriasis, rashes, burns and acne. It is known to be antiseptic, antifungal, antibacterial and antiviral, and is used in shampoo to control dandruff and lice.

Neem

Neem oil

Olives

Passionflower oil
(passionfruit, maracuja)

Passiflora incarnata

Extracted from the fruit and seeds of the passionflower, this oil is high in linoleic acids and is easily absorbed into the skin helping to restore the skin's elasticity. It is high in antioxidants and is a useful healing and antibacterial oil for dry itchy skin or scalp. Ideal for face preparations, balms and lotion bars.

Pomegranate seed oil

Punica granatum

The seeds of the pomegranate fruit are packed with antioxidants that fight free radicals and skin ageing. The oil is used to moisturize and heal dry, mature, cracked skin. It also helps to fight lines, wrinkles and sunburn and to aid regeneration of skin cells by helping to strengthen and nourish the epidermis and promote the skin's elasticity.

Olive oil

Olea europaea

Grown mainly in the Mediterranean, olives create a green to golden brown coloured oil depending on the quality. It is a complex compound made of fatty acids and high in oleic acid, vitamin A, vitamin E (a natural antioxidant), vitamin K and other important vitamins and minerals. The properties of olive oil are helpful for burns, inflammation, arthritis, wounds and dry skin. This oil makes a good carrier oil and base for balms.

Peach kernel oil

Prunus persica

This oil is easily absorbed into the skin and makes a good carrier or bath oil. Its properties are very similar to those of sweet almond oil.

Pomegranate

Pumpkin seeds

Raspberry

Rosemary extract

Rosmarinus officinalis

This is not actually an oil, but an extract from the rosemary plant. Rosemary extract is rich in antioxidants and when added to your recipes can help prolong the life of the product.

Rice bran oil

Oryza sativa

Extracted from the germ and inner husk of rice, rice bran oil is a mild and softening oil that has long been used in Japan to protect and moisturize mature or sensitive skin. Rich in essential fatty acids, vitamin E, oleic and linoleic acid, it has excellent antioxidant properties and helps inflamed, dry and ageing skin.

Pumpkin seed oil

Cucurbita pepo seed

This oil is made by pressing roasted, hulled pumpkin seeds and is usually a very dark green colour, sometimes referred to as 'green gold'. It is an extremely nutritious and nourishing oil, containing many important active constituents. High in essential fatty acids, omega 3, omega 6, vitamins A, C and E and zinc, pumpkin oil helps diminish stretch marks and wrinkles.

Raspberry seed oil

Rubus idaeus

Extracted from the seeds of the raspberry fruit. Raspberry seed oil is an excellent antioxidant, high in essential fatty acids and vitamin E, which plays an important role in the repair of skin damage. Its anti-inflammatory properties are superior to those of many other oils, and it is particularly useful in facial skincare as an emollient and to soothe the symptoms of eczema, rashes and overheated, irritated skin. Raspberry seed oil is reputed to act as a UV filter and is a valuable ingredient in sunscreens.

Rice

Rosehip

Sunflower seed

St John's Wort

Rosehip oil

Rosa canina fruit oil or *Rosa moschata seed oil*

Obtained from the seeds of rose hips, which contain high levels of vitamin E, this oil also contains retinol (vitamin A) and other essential fatty acids, which help delay the effects of skin ageing. It is widely used in skincare products for its regenerating properties, and is known to help dry, damaged, scarred skin, pigmentation and stretch marks. An oil perfect for face preparations.

Sunflower oil

Helianthus annuus

Produced from the seeds of the large well-known flower, this oil is packed with vitamins A, D and E, minerals, lecithin and essential fatty acids, and is ideal for soothing mature, dry skin and damaged, sensitive skin. Sunflower oil is easily absorbed into the skin and is therefore useful for massage and bath oils. It has a short shelf life of around three to six months, so it should be refrigerated once opened.

St John's Wort

Hypericum perforatum

A macerated oil infused with St. John's Wort herb, which is known to be antiseptic, healing and pain-relieving. This oil is known to ease nerve pain, neuralgia, sciatica, backache, shingles, lumbago, and is also helpful for sunburn, burns, damaged skin, wounds and ulcers.

Strawberry

Sweet almond oil

Prunus dulcis

This oil is pressed from the kernels of the sweet almond fruit and has been prized since ancient times. It contains vitamins A, B1, B2, B6 and E, making it a wonderful emollient that is used to nourish, protect and condition the skin, calm skin irritation, and soften dry skin. It is one of the most versatile oils, is easily absorbed into the skin and makes an excellent carrier oil.

Wheatgerm

Strawberry seed oil

Fragaria vesca or *Fragaria ananassa seed*

Containing some of the most powerful sources of antioxidants found in nature, this luxurious oil is high in gamma tocopherol and is a valuable source of essential fatty acids such as linoleic, alpha-linoleic and oleic acid, making it a wonderful anti-ageing ingredient. Highly emollient with a light texture and a subtle aroma, this oil is effective in helping dry and damaged skin. An expensive oil, but useful in lip balms and face preparations.

Vitamin E oil

Tocopherol

Vitamin E is a fat-soluble antioxidant found in a wide variety of fruit and vegetables and known to protect against cell-damaging free radicals. It is also effective in helping to reduce the appearance of stretch marks, age spots, scars, lines and wrinkles. This oil is dark, thick and viscous and is only used in small amounts to enhance a product or to help with oxidization.

Wheatgerm oil

Triticum vulgare

An emollient oil expressed from the germ of the wheat kernel. Wheatgerm oil is high in essential fatty acid, vitamins E, A, D, and linoleic acid (omega-6). A nourishing and skin-conditioning oil that helps the repair of sun-damaged, dehydrated and sensitive skin. It is known for its antioxidant properties which help to detoxify and protect the skin from environmental pollutants.

Beauty butters

What is a beauty butter?

A 'butter' is a naturally sourced, hard vegetable fat obtained from the kernels, or nuts, of plants that are solid at room temperature. The term is slightly misleading as these butters do not have anything to do with the dairy products normally associated with the word butter; they just have a similar creamy texture.

Butters such as cocoa, illippe, kokum, mango, murumuru, sal (shorea) and shea occur naturally and are obtained directly from the plant. Other vegetable-derived butters, such as coffee, hemp and macadamia, are obtained by first cold-processing and refining the fruits. The resulting oil leaves behind unsaponifiable matter – natural waxes and fatty fractions that cannot be mixed with alkalai and used to create soap. The unsaponifiable matter contains vitamins and moisturizing properties. It is blended with hydrogenated oil to produce a butter. High in healthy essential fatty acids, vitamins and minerals, these butters are a luxurious ingredient in the cosmetics and body-care industries.

The following butters can be gently melted until they are liquid and then added to body butters, balms, bath melts, soaps and bath bombs. Most butters can also be used on their own and will melt on contact with the skin (with the exception of some of the harder, high-melt-point oils such as cocoa, illipe and kokum.

Most butters should last for one or two years after purchase if they are kept in the right conditions, sometimes more. They generally have a low melt point and should therefore be stored in a cool place when it is warm. Ask your supplier for storage times and always store in an airtight container to prevent oxidization.

Note: Do not expect oils or butters to smell of the original fruit or plant, such as mango butter or raspberry oil, as the scent is not usually retained. However, each butter will still have its unique aroma. Make allowances for this as the aroma could alter the scent of your finished product.

Mango butter

Directory of butters

Aloe butter

Cocos nucifera (coconut) oil and Aloe barbadensis

Aloe butter is an extraction of aloe vera combined with coconut oil. The excellent properties of aloe are legendary in promoting the healing process and for treating dehydrated or sunburnt skin, eczema, psoriasis and windburn. The butter is very soft, so can be applied directly to the skin, where it will melt on contact.

Aloe butter

Avocado butter

Persea gratissima

A rich soft butter obtained from the crushed flesh of the sub-tropical avocado fruit. It is rich in vitamins A, B1, B2, D, and E and provides a wonderfully nourishing and hydrating treatment with natural sunscreen properties. Avocado butter melts very easily and is beneficial for dry, wrinkled skin or for damaged hair.

Cocoa butter

Theobroma cacao

One of the most common and also versatile butters. Cocoa butter is the fatty component of chocolate, produced from the fruit of the *Theobroma cacao* tree. Theobroma means 'food of the gods' and any chocoholic will understand why. Cocoa solids (chocolate powder) and cocoa butter are separated at the early stages of production for use in different manufacturing processes.

It is possible to purchase unrefined cocoa butter, which has a dark creamy colour and a fantastic chocolaty aroma.

The more widely available cocoa butter is the white, refined type that has no smell. This is useful if you want the many nutrients cocoa butter provides without the chocolaty smell.

Cocoa butter is a fairly hard butter, which is used in many cosmetic products such as bath melts, balms, body butters, soaps and bath bombs. It is known to provide a protective barrier to retain the moisture in your skin. It is also a source of natural antioxidants, which help ease dry skin and wrinkles; it is therefore often used in suntan lotions and skincare products.

Cocoa pods

Coffee beans

Cupuacu butter

Theobroma grandiflorum

Derived from an Amazonian tree, this creamy soft butter has exceptional water absorption and moisturizing properties, making it an effective ingredient for hair products. It also helps protect from UV-A and UV-B rays, restores elasticity to the skin and eases eczema and psoriasis.

Illipe butter

Shorea stenoptera

A butter made from the nuts of the Illipe tree, which is native to South East Asia and Borneo. This butter has similar properties to cocoa butter, it is highly moisturizing and has a high melting point, making it a useful ingredient for balms, bath melts and soap.

Coffee butter

Coffea arabica

A light brown butter with a delicious roasted coffee aroma and made from hydrogenated coffee bean oil. It offers natural sunscreen protection and provides excellent moisture retention to leave the skin wonderfully smooth. This is an excellent butter for lip balms and body butters.

Hemp seed butter

Cannabis sativa

Made from pressed hemp seeds and the natural waxes or fatty fractions from hempseed oil combined with hydrogenated oil. This butter is very high in essential fatty acids, and is often used in sunscreen preparations as it helps to protect the skin. A highly moisturizing and nourishing butter, it is non-greasy and easily absorbed into the skin. It is effective on dry, damaged skin, eczema and psoriasis, and used in lip balms and body butters.

Kokum butter

Garcinia indica

Similar to cocoa butter with a high melt point, making it perfect for lip balms, foot treatments, body butters and soaps. Rich in vitamin E, kokum butter soothes dry rough skin and wrinkles and restores the skin's elasticity.

Macadamia butter

Macadamia ternifolia

This butter is made by combining natural waxes or fatty fractions from macadamia nut oil as well as hydrogenated macadamia nut oil. It is a highly absorbent, moisturizing and nourishing butter providing excellent skin protection.

Mango butter

Mangifera indica

Tropical mango trees are mainly grown in Burma, Southern Asia and Northern India, mango butter is obtained from the fruit kernels of the tree. The butter is used for many applications including treating dry, sunburnt skin, providing protection from the sun, and treating wounds, rough skin, scars, wrinkles, eczema, psoriasis and dermatitis.

Olive

Mango butter

Murumuru butter

Astrocaryum murumuru

This is a highly nutritious and moisturizing butter sourced from the edible fruits of an Amazonian tree. It has a high oleic content and is rich in vitamin A with anti-inflammatory properties. Due to its water-retaining properties, it can be used in sunscreen products, hair-conditioning treatments and lip balms to provide a healthy gloss and shine.

Olive butter

Olea europea

Obtained from cold-pressed olives, with all the legendary properties of olive oil. It has a low melt point and can be used on its own, massaged directly into the skin, or added to balms, body butters, bath bombs and soaps.

Sal (Shorea) butter

Shorea robusta

Obtained from the fruit of the shorea robusta or shala tree, sal butter is a firm but pliable butter similar to mango or cocoa butter. It is high in oleic acids and extremely emollient, ideal for helping to restore flexibility in dry and wrinkled skin. It also has excellent oxidative stability, which is useful for lip balms and body butters.

Soya beans

Almond

Shea butter

Butyrospermum parkii

This naturally rich and creamy butter is obtained from the fruit of the African karite tree. Shea butter is highly emollient, rich in nutrients and has been prized for centuries by traditional African healers for its anti-ageing and moisturizing properties. It is used to help diminish the appearance of skin blemishes including scars, stretch marks, burns, rashes and eczema. The most luxurious shea butter is unrefined, retaining all of the plant's abundant nutrients. Unrefined shea butter is very rich and creamy with a strong nutty flavour and a relatively strong fragrance. If you wish to use a less odorous shea butter, choose the whiter, refined version.

Soy butter

Glycine soja

A soft butter obtained from soya beans, high in essential fatty acids and vitamin E. It has a smooth texture and absorbs easily into the skin making it an excellent moisturizer for dry, mature or chapped skin and a useful additive for lotion or massage bars, lip balms and hair-care products.

Shea butter

Sweet almond butter

Prunus amygdalus dulcis

A vegetable-derived butter usually derived from Mediterranean almonds with all the wonderful properties of sweet almond oil. This soft butter has excellent spreadability and is easily absorbed into the skin, leaving dry, cracked and chapped skin hydrated and with elasticity restored. It is used in balms, lotion or massage bars and sun-care preparations.

Waxes

For the recipes in this book, beeswax is used to make lip balms, body balms, hand salves and ointments. The hardness of wax, melted and added to a liquid oil, is used to solidify the mixture making it easier to transport and to apply, as well as providing the skin with nutrients and a natural protective barrier.

Beeswax is a natural product produced in the hive of the honey bee. Up to 100,000 bees can live in one beehive, the majority of these are female 'worker' bees who make wax honeycomb cells to raise young bees and to store honey (food) for the winter. When the cells are full of honey, the bees cap them with wax that is then scraped off by beekeepers to extract the honey. These clean wax cappings, together with some of the wax from the comb, are refined and used for candlemaking and cosmetics.

How is beeswax made?

When the temperature is right, the worker bees gorge themselves with honey (or sugar syrup) and cluster together at a temperature of 95°F (35°C). After 24 hours they secrete liquid wax through the membranes of four pairs of mirror-like glands on their abdomen. As the wax hardens, the bee moves it to her mouth, where it is chewed and mixed with glandular secretions. This soft wax is then passed from bee to bee and used for moulding the honeycomb.

During the nineteenth century, this assiduous creature rightly became the symbol of achievement and hard work in British heraldry, giving us the expression 'busy as a bee'.

Beekeepers inspecting a hive

History and application

Since the Middle Ages, beeswax has been used to make candles, but there are many other applications – particularly when it is blended with different minerals such as resins and polymers. Beeswax is used to produce waterproofing, cosmetics (lipstick, mascara, creams and balms), wax seals, wood or leather polish, lost wax casting, crayons, coatings for cheese, depilatory (hair removal) waxes, mould casting, surf and skating boards, in the manufacture of contact lenses and to create teeth impressions for dental work and wax models.

Since medieval times, wax chandlers were responsible for the preparation, production and selling of beeswax and its related products, which were commonly used by the church, the court and by the nobility. Its uses included forms of lighting such as tapers, torches and candles, wax images and moulding, wax for the medical profession, embalming and wax writing tablets and seals. Wax seals were used as proof that a letter had not been opened. It also authenticated the sender through the impression of a coat of arms or insignia in the wax, hence the expression 'seal of approval'. Wax seals are still sometimes used today, mainly for important legal or ceremonial documents.

The only beeswax refinery now operating in the UK is the British Wax Refining Company, which has a long history of refining and processing natural waxes. It all started in 1899 when Sidney Charles Case-Green joined the Beeswax Company Ltd of Liverpool in 1899 where he gained his expert knowledge of waxes. Sidney then founded his own company for the purpose of bleaching and refining wax. Under the leadership of Sidney's sons the business grew and they supplied companies such as the famous London wax figure museum, Madame Tussauds, whom they still supply to this day. The family business continued with Sidney's grandsons and is now run by his great grandchildren who continue to seek and develop new applications for wax.

White beeswax pellets

Yellow beeswax

Vegetable waxes

The following waxes are vegan alternatives to beeswax and are all obtained from plants. They are useful for use in lip balms, body balms, salves, ointments and lotion or massage bars. Simply heat and use them as you would beeswax, although you may need to experiment a little with quantities to achieve the desired consistency of your final products.

- Almond wax *Prunus amygdalus dulcis*
- Candelilla wax *Euphorbia cerifera*
- Carnauba wax *Copernicia cerifera*
- Hemp wax *Cannabis sativa*
- Jojoba wax *Simmondsia chinensis*
- Olive wax *Olea europaea*
- Rice bran wax *Oryza sativa*

Almond wax pellets

Carnauba wax pellets

Jojoba wax pellets

Olive wax pellets

Herbs and botanicals

For thousands of years, plant essences, botanicals, herbs, resins and aromatic oils have been used by civilizations to heal, purify, beautify, prevent disease and for worship.

Herbs from flowers, fruits, leaves, stems and roots have been used for centuries in different herbal medicine practices including Chinese, Ayurvedic, Siddha and Tibb Unani. Such is the belief in the power of the plant, that these therapies are still practised and highly valued today. Other complementary therapies that use nature's ingredients (flowers, herbs, oils and gums) such as aromatherapy, herbalism, flower remedies and homeopathy play an increasingly important part in healthcare alongside modern medicine. However, it is important to note that these are 'complementary' therapies and should not be used in place of conventional medical advice and treatment.

Ancient art and manuscripts show that herbs were used in important religious ceremonies and banquets, in incense and sacrifice, and to anoint brave travellers on their journeys. Certain herbs were so valued by the Romans that they took them on their travels; these particular plants have been found in archaeological sites around the world. In ancient times aromatic herbal oils, resins and plant essences were regarded as more valuable than gold and were often presented as gifts. The precious oils you owned and adorned your body with were evidence of your wealth.

Some people believe that locked within the plants is the ability to heal and cure. Yet with the destruction of many forests and the flora and fauna that grows beneath their canopies, these potential cures for illness and disease are disappearing. It is therefore wise to purchase not only the best ingredients, but those ethically sourced from sustainable sources.

Macerated oils

Herbs can be macerated (infused) in a carrier oil thereby releasing the volatile oils contained within the plant and adding many of the plant's therapeutic properties to the carrier oil. These oils can be applied directly to the skin or added to balms, oils, butters, soaps or bath bombs. You can either select a herb from the following list and make your own macerated oil, or you can purchase macerated oils from many of the suppliers listed in the back of this book (see page 149) or others via the internet. Dried herbs can also be added directly to your soaps and bath bombs.

Common macerated oils

Arnica

Arnica montana

Used for bruises, swellings, muscle pain, backache, sore joints, pulled muscles, sore ligaments or cartilage. It is often used as a muscle rub or bath oil after sport and for people with arthritis or rheumatism. Do not use on broken skin.

Calendula (Marigold)

Calendula officinalis

The orange-yellow petals of the marigold are a traditional remedy for minor skin problems such as cuts, wounds and grazes. As well as providing beneficial skin-conditioning properties, these sunny yellow petals are the only flowers that retain their colour in soap. They are also an attractive additive to bath treats. Calendula has long been used to help inflamed skin conditions such as acne and sunburn and as a herbal remedy for athlete's foot, thrush and fungal conditions. Marigold has been used historically to help prevent infections spreading and to speed up the process of cell regeneration.

Comfrey

Symphytum officinale

A hairy-leafed plant with light purple, cream or pink flowers related to borage and forget-me-nots. Famously known as 'knitbone' for its ability to 'knit' or heal the flesh, comfrey contains a natural compound called allantoin, which promotes cell healing and the growth of healthy tissue, soothing, protecting and softening the skin. Comfrey also contains mucilage, a gooey polymer that acts as a membrane thickener: it forms a soothing film over mucus membrane, thereby relieving pain and inflammation (mucilage is also found in aloe vera, cactus and marshmallow). Both the leaves and the roots are widely used in herbal medicine for healing broken bones, sprains, cuts, wounds, skin irritation and bruises and for easing pain, inflammation, haemorrhoids and gout.

Mullein

Verbascum thapsus

Mullein has been used historically in herbalism for helping to ease the symptoms of bronchitis, congestion, coughs and sore throats. Its rehydrating and moisturizing properties make it a useful additive to lip balms and salves. It is also used to help treat scrapes, minor abrasions and haemorrhoid pain.

St John's Wort

Hypericum perforatum

Traditionally used to treat inflamed nerves, neuralgia, sciatica, sprains, burns, sunburn, wounds and bruises. It is also used as an anti-inflammatory and for treating acne, spots and sensitive inflamed skin. In rare cases St John's Wort can increase photosensitivity, so avoid exposure to the sun when using this herb.

Comfrey

Directory of herbs and additives

As well as the common herbs used in macerated oils, the following ingredients can be added to soaps and bath bombs or infused, then strained, into your bath oils and balms for extra therapeutic benefits, decoration or colour.

Burdock

Arctium lappa

Belonging to the thistle group, both the leaf and root of the plant are used. Their seed pods, with their natural hook and loop fasteners that enable the seed to be attached to animals, were apparently the inspiration for the modern-day invention of fasteners made of nylon. The herb is well used as a blood purifier, to minimize boils, acne, eczema, and ulcers, and to ease inflamed skin.

Chamomile

Anthemis nobilis

A strongly aromatic white flower with a yellow centre, very much like a daisy. Chamomile is an old favourite amongst garden herbs. The dried flowers are a pretty additive to floral or herbal bath bombs (the whole of the small flowers are yellow when dried) and the yellow powder will give your bath treat a pale yellow-tan colour. Chamomile has been used historically for its sedative and relaxing properties and is known to soothe sensitive and irritated skin.

Cocoa (chocolate) powder (or melted chocolate)

Theobrama cacao

Surely a must for all chocolate lovers. Cocoa is a great additive when it is combined with moisturizing cocoa butter, the fatty part of the cacao bean, which is separated from the solids at the beginning of the extraction process. Cocoa powder also contains natural antioxidants known to protect and nourish the skin. Add to soaps, bath bombs, truffles, melts or balms.

Burdock

Chamomile flowers

Cocoa powder

Bladderwrack (seaweed)

Fucus vesiculosus

Bladderwrack is a large nutrient-rich sea plant, commonly referred to as 'seaweed'. Abundant in amino acids, iodine and vitamins, it was first used by the ancient Greeks who maximized its anti-inflammatory, anti-fungal, anti-bacterial, anti-viral, antioxidant and antiseptic properties. Bladderwrack is used to tone, detox, moisturize, revitalize the skin and to boost immunity.

Green tea

Camellia sinensis

Green tea has been used in China, Japan, India and Thailand for centuries for assisting digestion, lowering blood sugar and for healing wounds. It is known to be a powerful antioxidant containing a wide variety of vitamins and minerals that help to protect the skin. It is also known to have skin-rejuvenating and healing properties and has been used to help athlete's foot, bedsores and skin disease.

Honey

Mel

Honey is a food source produced by the honey bee, obtained from the nectar of different flora and fauna. It is a mixture of sugars and other compounds, vitamins and minerals. The exact composition of each honey will vary according to the different mix of flower nectars obtained. Add to soaps or balms. It is best to warm honey slightly before adding to soap to ensure even distribution.

Powdered bladderwrack

Green tea

Honey

Lemon balm

Melissa officinalis

With its heart-shaped, deliciously lemon-scented leaves, lemon balm can be used as a substitute for lemons in cookery dishes. This balm was an ingredient in Carmelite water or 'Eau de Carmes', a perfumed toilet water created by Carmelite Monks in the seventeenth century, which was taken internally to ease nervous headaches and neuralgia. It is effective for the nervous system, depression, memory, headaches, herpes, insomnia, colds and fevers, and insect bites.

Milk thistle

Silybum marianum

Rich in essential fatty acids, milk thistle is a powerful antioxidant. It contains silymarin, which is known to decrease inflammation and to help combat free radicals. It is best known for its ability to heal the liver. As certain skin conditions are thought to result from liver malfunction, milk thistle is often recommended for topical use to aid liver problems.

Nettle

Urtica dioica

The stinging hairs on this herbaceous flowering plant has given it the name 'stinging nettle'. The leaves are high in nutrients such as vitamins A, C and D, iron, potassium, manganese, calcium and nitrogen, and once cooked or crushed, the chemicals in the leaves that cause the sting will be destroyed. Similar to mallow and comfrey, nettle contains the emollient 'mucilage' as well as minerals, formic acid, beta-carotene and phosphates. Nettle is used as an astringent and a stimulating tonic, particularly for the hair. As a diuretic it stimulates the kidneys and bladder and detoxifies the body. It is known to ease the symptoms of gout and arthritis and to stimulate the immune system.

Lemon balm

Milk thistle

Nettle

Oats

Avena sativa

Oats are the seed of a cereal grain, the extract of which is used in many topical skincare applications for eczema and psoriasis. Historically, it has been used to help manage dry and itchy skin conditions. The addition of rolled or ground oats to your soap base can create a wonderful texture and provide a gentle exfoliation, leaving the skin soft and silky.

Rooibos (Redbush) tea

Aspalathus linearis

A caffeine-free red herbal tea unique to the Cedarberg mountains in South Africa. The reddish-brown needle-like leaves are packed with antioxidants, and have been used historically in South Africa to relieve eczema, skin disorders and inflammation and to boost the immune system. Added to soap it gives an attractive fleck, texture and natural colour to the bars.

Rose

Rosa canina

A few rose petals or buds can be used to decorate soaps, bath bombs, or truffles, or to add a special touch to bottles of body oil. However, the buds and petals will lose their colour over time, particularly if they are left in direct light. Additionally, do not add petals directly into your soap mix as the petals will turn brown.

Rolled oats

Rooibos tea

Rose buds

Essential oils

Essential oils are the spirit, personality or essence of an aromatic plant. They are the fragrant, natural volatile liquids found in plants, leaves, fruit, seeds, roots, wood, resin, rum, grasses and flowers.

On a hot day, plants release their oils into the air, either as protection from pests and infection or to attract bees and insects for pollination. Essential oils are widely used in the practice of aromatherapy to help ease a multitude of complaints and conditions. Many are known to be antiseptic,

antiviral, antifungal and antibacterial. At the same time they can affect your mood and well-being, helping to relax both the body and mind.

It can take a huge amount of raw material to obtain even a small amount of these precious volatile oils, so large areas of crops are required. Different extraction methods are used to obtain the essential oils of plants, which are held in special cells within the plant tissues: these include steam distillation, expression, solvent extraction or the carbon dioxide method.

Aromatherapy

Aromatherapy is a form of holistic practice of caring for the body. Essential oils are applied in several ways including massage, inhalation, vaporization, compresses, bath products and skincare, to help improve physical, mental and emotional health. Aromatherapy has become one of the most enjoyable and popular complementary therapies in recent times.

The term 'aromathérapie' was created in the 1920s by a French Chemist, René-Maurice Gattefossé. It literally means a therapy using aromas. Gattefossé is reputed to have discovered the healing and antiseptic properties of essential oils when he burned his arm and cooled it down with lavender oil, the substance closest to hand. The pain relief and speedy healing that followed prompted him to spend his life researching the subject.

In 1964 another Frenchman, Dr Jean Valnet, carried out further research into the healing properties of oils on wounded soldiers and published his well-known aromatherapists' bible *The Practice of Aromatherapy*.

The olfactory sense is one of the first to develop and a smell can instantly remind us of a childhood memory or place from the past. Aromas can trigger a change in our mood: imagine how a stroll in a fragrant rose garden can lift and calm the spirits, while a walk down a garbage-strewn alleyway promotes an unpleasant feeling, thereby lowering the spirits. The aroma of essential oils is believed to have the same effect on mood: simply by breathing in the floral aroma of lavender we begin to feel relaxed, calm and de-stressed, while the scent of lemons can awaken our senses and invigorate and refresh the mind.

A warm bath is one of the most pleasurable ways to use essential oils, as the complex chemical compounds they contain are believed to enter the bloodstream through the skin. The blissful sensation of surrounding your body with aromatic scent is one of the most effective ways of unwinding and letting go of the day's tension and stresses.

Some therapeutic uses of essential oils

Stretch marks and scars	mandarin, neroli, patchouli, tangerine, vetiver, benzoin, elemi and manuka
Babies, pregnancy	rose geranium, lavender, chamomile, yarrow and mandarin
Antibacterial	tea tree, manuka, lavender, lemon, marjoram and thyme
Dry scalp	bay, lavender, lemongrass, rosemary, tea tree, manuka, chamomile, myrrh, patchouli, peppermint and ylang ylang
Sunburn	chamomile, lavender
Cellulite	black pepper, cypress, grapefruit, juniper, lime, orange, mandarin, tangerine and rosemary
Mental clarity	bergamot, citronella, lemon, lime, juniper, grapefruit, pine, rosemary, peppermint and ginger
Aphrodisiac, sensual	black pepper, cardamom, clary sage, ginger, jasmine, patchouli, sandalwood, vetiver and ylang ylang
Headaches	cajeput, dill, lavender, lime, may chang, orange, peppermint, rosemary, lemongrass, chamomile, coriander and marjoram
Insomnia	chamomile, clary sage, lavender, mandarin, marjoram, melissa, neroli, petitgrain, vetiver and yarrow
PMT and painful periods	clary sage, fennel, geranium, cardamom, chamomile, jasmine and vetiver
Detox	cypress, fennel, grapefruit, juniper, lemon and orange

Colds, flu, bronchitis, coughs, congestion	mandarin, neroli, patchouli, tangerine, vetiver, benzoin, frankincense, fennel, elemi and manuka
Mental and physical exhaustion or fatigue	coriander, cinnamon, petitgrain, sandalwood, vetiver, cardamom, hyssop, nutmeg and yarrow
Anxiety, depression, stress, relaxation	benzoin, bergamot, chamomile, clary sage, frankincense, lavender, lemongrass, myrrh, mandarin, may chang, orange, palmarosa, petitgrain, rose geranium, tangerine, vetiver, yarrow and ylang ylang
Muscle aches and pains, rheumatism, arthritis	cypress, ginger, juniper, lavender, nutmeg, benzoin, black pepper, clary sage, peppermint, petitgrain, tea tree, thyme, cajeput, bay, benzoin, cedarwood, cinnamon, eucalyptus, citronella, hyssop, lemon, lime, marjoram, pine and vetiver
Digestion, flatulence, constipation	black pepper, fennel, grapefruit, orange, cardamom, ginger, hyssop, lemon, lemongrass, mandarin, marjoram, peppermint, petitgrain and rosemary
Eczema, psoriasis	benzoin, cedarwood, lavender, myrrh, patchouli, palmarosa, rose geranium, geranium and sandalwood
Dry, mature skin	elemi, neroli, benzoin, geranium, rose geranium, jasmine, patchouli, sandalwood, frankincense and myrrh
Oily skin	bog myrtle, cajeput, cedarwood, citronella, geranium, grapefruit, juniper, lemon, lime, mandarin, may chang, tea tree and ylang ylang
Acne	benzoin, bog myrtle, cedarwood, grapefruit, juniper, lemon, lime, may chang, patchouli, palmarosa, tea tree, thyme and vetiver
Fungal infections, athlete's foot, feet	tea tree, manuka, citronella, myrrh, thyme and lemongrass

Safety

Essential oils should never be used neat and applied directly to the skin. Always add to a carrier oil, bath bomb, soap or balm. They are very potent; we therefore advise that the amounts stated in the recipes should not be exceeded. Certain oils should not be used over certain percentages, so care should be taken to read the information given on each essential oil before making your own recipes.

These oils should not be taken internally and must be kept away from young children and animals at all times. If they are accidentally swallowed, seek medical help immediately. If any oils get into the eyes, irrigate with water immediately and if symptoms persist seek medical advice. Although essential oils (aromatherapy oils) have been historically used to ease various medical conditions, aromatherapy is a complementary therapy and should in no way be substituted for medical advice.

If you suffer from allergies, we advise using a test patch or immersing a small part of your body in the water before climbing into the bath. Essential oils from some citrus fruits may react with sunlight. Avoid exposure to sunlight or ultraviolet (UV) light for 12 hours after using orange, lemon, lemongrass, grapefruit, bergamot, petitgrain, lime, mandarin, tangerine and dill as these are phototoxic (can react with sunlight).

Most essential oils should be avoided by children under the age of seven; the exceptions are lavender, geranium, chamomile, mandarin, and yarrow, and these should be used in quantities no more than 0.5%. The recipes in the book are therefore intended for use by people aged seven and above unless specified otherwise.

Safety measures

Advice from a qualified practitioner or medical adviser should be sought if you:

- have a known medical condition, such as high blood pressure or epilepsy
- are receiving any psychiatric or medical treatment
- are taking medication
- are pregnant or breast-feeding
- wish to treat young children

Storage

Essential oils should be stored in dark-coloured glass jars or bottles in a cool environment. Many oils can last for years if stored in this way, however citrus oils will generally lose their properties approximately one year after purchase. As with perfumes, exposure to oxygen will quickly degrade essential oils, so make sure that there is as little space between the surface of the oil and the top of the bottle as possible.

These oils can also damage clothing and wooden surfaces, so cover yourself and any surfaces before using them.

Directory of essential oils

There are too many essential oils to list in this book, but the following are the most common, current and useful oils with brief descriptions of each. The letter after the name of each oil denotes whether it is a top **(T)**, middle **(M)** or base note **(B)**.

(T, M) indicates a top to middle note that may be used as either. The section on perfume (see pages 33–37) contains information on perfume notes and how to blend your own therapeutic perfume for use in your own recipes.

Bay (T, M)
Pimenta racemosa

Fragrance: sweet, spicy and fresh with a balsamic undertone.

Known uses: muscular aches and pains, rheumatism, neuralgia, circulation problems, colds, flu and viral infections, hair and scalp treatments, dandruff, hair growth, skin infections.

Blends with: cedarwood, eucalyptus, geranium, coriander, ginger, rosemary, juniper, lavender, orange, lemon, thyme and ylang ylang.

Bay leaves and buds

Benzoin (B)
Styrax benzoin

Fragrance: warm, sweet vanilla-like scent with a treacle-like viscosity.

Known uses: Benzoin is a tree resin and can be used as a fixative or a preservative. Calming, uplifting and comforting. Circulation, chilblains, dry and cracked skin, respiratory disorders, sores, wounds, acne, scar tissue, eczema, rheumatism, arthritis, circulation, stress, nervous tension and muscle pains.
Caution: limit to 0.5%.

Blends with: coriander, bergamot, frankincense, lemon, lavender, juniper, myrrh and orange.

Bergamot (T, M)
Citrus bergamia

Fragrance: sweet, fresh, with a bright citrus scent and a warm floral quality.

Known uses: Bergamot is a small bitter orange from Lombardy in Italy best-known for its flavouring of Earl Grey tea. It is also one of the main ingredients in Eau de Cologne. Useful for boosting your spirits and immunity, stress and depression, colds and flu, thrush, urinary tract infection.
Caution: strongly phototoxic, use sparingly – max use 0.5%.

Blends with: jasmine, cypress, neroli, lavender, black pepper, frankincense, geranium, mandarin, nutmeg, orange, rosemary, sandalwood, vetiver, clary sage and ylang ylang.

Black pepper (M)

Piper nigrum

Fragrance: fresh, warm, sharp, spicy dry-woody smell.

Known uses: One of the oldest known spices, used in India over 4,000 years ago. Useful for digestion, colds and flu, immune system, circulation, cellulite, aches and pains, rheumatism, muscle relaxant, aphrodisiac.

Caution: not recommended to be used in concentrations of more than 1%.

Blends with: sandalwood, ginger, lime, frankincense, juniper, rosemary, neroli, cardamom, fennel, cedarwood, clove, bergamot, bergamot, clary sage, fennel, coriander, geranium, grapefruit, lavender, lemon, mandarin, sage and ylang ylang.

Bog myrtle (T,M)

Myrica gale

Fragrance: clear, fresh sweet, camphoraceous, herbaceous scent, slightly menthol.

Known uses: Also known as 'sweet gale', bog myrtle is native to northern Europe and North America and has properties similar to tea tree oil. It is enjoying a revival in skincare products for its anti-ageing properties and its use for sensitive skin, oily skin, open pores and acne. Also useful for depression, poor memory, to promote well-being, repel insects and, before the use of hops, to flavour beer.

Blends with: lemon, juniper, lime, cypress, lavender and tea tree.

Cajeput (T)

Melaleuca leucadendron cajuputi

Fragrance: sweet, camphoraceous, penetrating medicinal smell.

Known uses: colds, flu, bronchitis, laryngitis, sinusitis, asthma, headaches, earache, rheumatism, gout, arthritis, muscular aches and pains, antiseptic, deodorizing, insect repellent/bites, oily skin, itchy scalp, urinary system, intestinal problems.

Blends with: angelica, bergamot, cardamom, clove, eucalyptus, geranium, juniper, lavender, nutmeg and thyme.

Cardamom (M)

Elettaria cardamomum

Fragrance: warm, fruity, sweet and spicy aromatic scent with a pungent freshness and woody, floral undertones.

Known uses: Related botanically to ginger, cardamom has been used in traditional Chinese and Indian Ayurvedic medicine for over 3,000 years as a tonic for the lungs and for its immune-boosting properties. Also useful for digestion, nausea, heartburn, coughs, flatulence, bad breath caused by gastric problems, mental fatigue, aphrodisiac and as a general tonic.

Blends with: rosemary, frankincense, sandalwood, ylang ylang, bergamot, cinnamon and cedarwood.

Cardamon pods

Black peppercorns

Cedarwood

Chamomile

Cedarwood (B)

Cedrus atlantica or *Juniperus virginiana*

Fragrance: clean, sharp and fresh with slightly sweet, woody, balsamic undertones.

Known uses: Cedarwood is a native tree of North America, the oil is distilled from wood chips and sawdust and was historically used as medicine by the Native Americans. The Egyptians also used the oil as an insect repellent and for mummification. Useful for acne, arthritis, rheumatism, bronchitis, nervous tension, eczema, oily skin, cystitis and urinary infections.

Blends with: bergamot, cinnamon, cypress, frankincense, juniper, lavender, lemon, neroli, myrrh, sandalwood, rose, jasmine, vetiver and rosemary.

Chamomile (Roman) (M)

Anthemis nobilis

Fragrance: refreshing, sweet, herbaceous, apple-like, fresh scent.

Known uses: This soothing, calming oil is pale blue in colour and is known as 'ground apple'. It is widely used in baby and children's products. It is also useful for inflammation, PMS, menstrual cramps, insomnia, migraine, restlessness, stress, allergies and hayfever.

Blends with: clary sage, bergamot, lavender, geranium, jasmine, tea tree, grapefruit, rose, lemon, rose, ylang ylang, marjoram and geranium.

Cinnamon leaf (T)

Cinnamomum zeylanicum

Fragrance: warm, spicy, musky aroma.

Known uses: antiseptic, antibacterial, viral infections, colds, flu, chills, aches and pains, immune system, rheumatism, digestive system, kidney problems. Not to be confused with cinnamon bark, which is a skin irritant and should not be used.

Caution: avoid during pregnancy and limit to 0.5%.

Blends with: ginger, frankincense, cardamom, grapefruit, coriander, thyme lavender and rosemary.

Citronella (T)

Cymbopogan nardus

Fragrance: warm, woody-sweet with a fresh lemony scent.

Known uses: The oil is extracted from a hardy grass, native to Sri Lanka and Java, and is very well-known insect repellent. Also useful for colds and flu, fever, minor infections, cuts, abrasions and swellings, oily skin, arthritis, neuralgia, rheumatism, muscular pain, deodorizing and as an antifungal treatment for feet.

Blends with: lemon, orange, pine, lavender, bergamot and geranium.

Clary sage (T, M)

Salvia sclarea

Fragrance: sweet, nutty, rich, herbaceous.

Known uses: muscle relaxant, depression, menstrual cramps, stress, nervous tension, insomnia, aphrodisiac.
Caution: do not use when pregnant or when drinking alcohol as it can cause drowsiness.

Blends with: juniper, lavender, lemon, pine, sandalwood, coriander, geranium, jasmine, frankincense and citrus oils.

Coriander seeds

Coriander (T,M)

Coriandrum sativum

Fragrance: sweet, spicy, musky fragrance with a peppery base note.

Known uses: neuralgia, rheumatic pains, muscular pains, joint pain, gout, flatulence, nausea, nervous exhaustion, anorexia nervosa, cold and flu, mental fatigue, migraine and nervous tension.

Blends with: orange, neroli, bergamot. lemon, grapefruit, ginger and cinnamon.

Cypress (M)

Cupressus sempervirens

Fragrance: smoky, nutty with a slight spiciness and sweet, resinous notes.

Known uses: Historically used as an incense ingredient and in aftershaves and colognes. Also useful for spasmodic coughs, bronchitis, lymphatic drainage, detoxifying, cellulite, water retention, soothing emotions, varicose veins, haemorrhoids, circulation and chilblains.

Blends with: juniper, pine, bergamot, clary sage, lavender, marjoram, rosemary, sandalwood, frankincense and citrus oils.

Cypress

Clary sage

Dill (T)

Anethum graveolens

Fragrance: light, fresh, warm, spicy scent, slightly resembling liquorice.

Known uses: stimulating, revitalizing, and balancing. Useful for digestion, intestinal spasms, bloating, constipation, flatulence, hiccoughs, healing of wounds, calming of the mind, excess sweating due to nervous tension, headaches, coughs, colds and flu.

Blends with: nutmeg, bergamot and citrus oils.

Elemi (M)

Canarium luzonicum

Fragrance: fresh, peppery, balsamic, rich, sweet and spicy.

Known uses: A resinous gum with a pleasant aroma that was used by the ancient Egyptians for embalming. Useful for bronchitis, catarrh, phlegm, healing of scars, immune system, emotional healing, mature skin, rough dry wrinkly skin and skin disorders.

Blends with: all citrus oils, cinnamon, clove, frankincense, lavender, myrrh and rosemary.

Eucalyptus (T)

Eucalyptus globulus

Fragrance: sharp, fresh, camphoraceous smell with slight woody undertones.

Known uses: Historically used as a medicinal herb by the Aborigines. Useful for fevers, colds, bronchitis, rheumatism, muscular aches and pains, urinary and genital infections.
Caution: must not be swallowed.

Blends with: cypress, lavender, thyme, lemon, marjoram, cedarwood, tea tree, lemongrass and pine.

Dill

Eucalyptus

Frankincense (B)

Boswellia carterii

Fragrance: fresh top note with sweet, woody, resinous undertones.

Known uses: A highly prized gum resin used as far back as the time of ancient Egypt for skincare and in incense for worship and fumigation of the sick. Also useful for meditation, stress, inflammation, damaged or ageing skin, toning, rejuvenating, anxiety, coughs, tension, bronchitis and laryngitis.

Blends with: basil, neroli, cedarwood, pine, sandalwood, myrrh, vetiver, rose geranium, lavender, orange, bergamot and lemon.

Fennel

Geranium

Frankincense

Fennel (T, M)

Foeniculum vulgare

Fragrance: spicy-sweet, green, herby aniseed-like scent.

Known uses: Well used in ancient times, it was cultivated by the Romans for courage and strength. Known as 'fenkle' in medieval times, it was used to ward off evil spirits. The modern name fennel comes from the Latin *foenum*, meaning hay. Useful for digestion, colitis, nausea, vomiting, diuretic, constipation, kidney stones, flatulence, bloatedness, nervous indigestion, obesity, coughs and bronchitis.

Caution: do not use if pregnant or epileptic, or in high concentrations.

Blends with: geranium, lavender, rose, marjoram and sandalwood.

Geranium (T, M)

Pelargonium graveolens

Fragrance: fresh top note with sweet, woody, resinous undertones.

Known uses: Widely used in skincare products and perfumery. Also useful for neuralgia, anxiety, depression, oily skin, hot flushes, dry or inflamed skin and as a toner, sedative, diuretic and an uplifting oil.

Blends with: any oil, especially lime, bergamot, marjoram, palmarosa, neroli, jasmine, grapefruit, sandalwood, orange, cedarwood, clary sage and rosemary.

Ginger (T, M)

Zingiber officinale

Fragrance: Hot, dry, pungent and musty with a lingering spicy sweetness.

Known uses: Ginger root has been traditionally used in Chinese medicine for digestion and circulation. It is also useful for colds and flu, fevers, the immune system, poor circulation, muscular pains, nausea and as an aphrodisiac.

Blends with: all citrus and spicy oils, particularly bergamot, juniper, neroli, rose geranium, frankincense, vetiver, sandalwood, ylang ylang and cedarwood.

Grapefruit (T)

Citrus grandis

Fragrance: fresh, zesty, sweet, citrus smell

Known uses: A good pick-me-up with a positive effect on the mind and helpful for those affected by SAD. Also useful for detoxifying, oily skin, acne, cellulite, constipation, hangovers, water retention, digestive, liver and kidney problems, immune system, colds and influenza.

Caution: limit to 1%.

Blends with: bergamot, frankincense, palmarosa, pine, geranium and eucalyptus.

Hyssop (T, M)

Hyssopus officinalis

Fragrance: sweet camphoraceous top note with a spicy, herbaceous warming undertone.

Known uses: respiratory problems, colds, flu, coughs, tonsillitis and catarrh, sore throats, bronchitis, digestion, bruises, flatulence, indigestion and colic, asthma, alertness, fatigue, rheumatism, blood pressure, grief and water-retention.

Caution: do not use if epileptic or if you are pregnant.

Blends with: geranium, orange, clary sage, melissa and rosemary.

Hyssop

Ginger root

Grapefruit

Jasmine

Juniper

Lavender (T, M)

Lavandula angustifolia

Fragrance: fresh, light, soft, clean sweet floral.

Known uses: Widely used in perfumery, lavender blends well with many other essential oils. It is an extremely useful oil with numerous therapeutic benefits. The most common uses are stress, pain, nervous tension, insomnia, headaches, neuralgia, eczema, psoriasis, thrush, bites, wounds, burns, stings, bites, shock and as an insect repellent.

Blends with: all oils.

Jasmine (M, B)

Jasminum officinale

Fragrance: rich, warm, sweet, exotic floral scent.

Known uses: Due to its importance in the perfume industry, jasmine is known as the 'king of oils'. The flowers are picked at night at just one day old. Useful for anxiety, depression, dry and sensitive skin, and as an aphrodisiac, labour pains, post-natal depression, and menstrual pain.

Blends with: bergamot, sandalwood and all citrus oils.

Juniper (M)

Juniperus communis

Fragrance: fresh, camphoraceous, woody, herbaceous smell.

Known uses: detox, digestion, urinary tract, diuretic, respiratory complaints, concentration, rheumatism, circulation, gout, oily skin and acne.

Blends with: cedarwood, bergamot, cypress, ginger, sandalwood, lavender, pine, rosemary and all citrus oils.

Lavender

Lemon (T)

Citrus medica limonum

Fragrance: sweet, green, citrus smell.

Known uses: tonic, diuretic, digestion, colds, flu, arthritis, immune system, acne, detox, lymphatic drainage, detox, boils, concentration, oily skin, rheumatism, arthritis, gout, abscesses, varicose veins, high blood pressure, and circulation.

Blends with: lavender, sandalwood, benzoin, eucalyptus, geranium, fennel, juniper and neroli.

Lemongrass (T, M)

Cymbopogon shoenanthus

Fragrance: herbaceous, sweet, zesty lemon scent.

Known uses: A fast-growing perennial grass from India used in complementary Ayurvedic medicine to help cool fevers and to treat infectious diseases. Also useful for digestion, migraine, respiratory conditions, fever, muscular aches and pains, constipation, depression, anxiety, nervous exhaustion, stress, athlete's foot, acne, jet lag and hangovers and as an insect repellent.

Caution: phototoxic.

Blends with: geranium, rosemary, tea tree, vetiver, cedarwood, coriander, jasmine, lavender, pine, eucalyptus, neroli, palmarosa and rosemary.

Lime (T)

Citrus aurantifolia

Fragrance: Sharp, fresh, zesty citrus peel aroma.

Known uses: Astringent, tonic, headaches, fevers, immune system, flu, bronchitis, sinusitis, clearing the mind, depression, circulation, cellulite, obesity, travel sickness, arthritis, rheumatism, oily skin and acne.

Caution: limit to 1%.

Blends with: juniper, neroli, lavender, clary sage, ylang ylang and citrus oils.

Lemon

Lime

Mandarin (T)

Citrus nobilis

Fragrance: Very sweet, rich, tangy, floral scent.

Known uses: As one of the most gentle oils, mandarin can be used by children, during pregnancy and for the elderly. Useful for calming children, stress, stretch marks, stomach cramps, nervous indigestion, oily skin, digestion, flatulence, diarrhoea, constipation, circulation, fluid retention, insomnia.

Caution: may be slightly phototoxic.

Blends with: lavender, frankincense, juniper, bergamot, clary sage, lavender and neroli.

Marjoram

Manuka

Marjoram (M)

Origanum marjorana

Fragrance: warm, woody, slightly spicy aroma.

Known uses: The name 'origanum' comes from the Greek language and means 'joy of the mountains'. Useful for muscular aches, insomnia, sedative, digestion, PMT, hypertension, rheumatism, arthritis, colds, bronchitis, migraine and nervous indigestion.

Blends with: lavender, bergamot, ginger, vetiver, cypress, cedarwood, chamomile, eucalyptus and tea tree.

Manuka (T, M)

Leptosperum scoparium

Fragrance: A sweet honey-like aroma, with woody, mossy notes.

Known uses: With its antibacterial, antifungal and anti-inflammatory properties, manuka oil has long been used by the Maori people of New Zealand as a medicinal herb. Manuka is so powerful that it has been introduced into hospitals to fight superbugs. Useful for cuts, nervous tension, spots, boils, ulcers, stress, anxiety, dry or sensitive skin.

Caution: limit to 1%.

Blends with: bergamot, black pepper, cedarwood, ginger, juniper, lavender, peppermint, rosemary, sandalwood, vetiver and ylang ylang.

Mandarin

May chang (T)

Litsea cubeba

Fragrance: intense lemony, sweet fresh and fruity note.

Known uses: A traditional Chinese herb used for centuries for medicinal purposes. This tropical and fragrant tree produces a small pepper-like fruit from which the oil is distilled. Useful for chills, headaches, muscular aches and pains, oily skin, acne, greasy skin, stress, anxiety, depression, antiseptic, antiperspirant and deodorizing.

Blends with: lavender, neroli, petitgrain, sandalwood, cedarwood, bergamot, ginger, rosemary, geranium, cypress, black pepper, cardamom and orange.

Melissa (Lemon balm/ Bee balm)

Melissa officinalis

Fragrance: fresh lemony, sweet citrus, herbaceous odour fresh and fruity.

Known uses: The name 'melissa' comes from the Greek word for bee as the plant is very attractive to them. The oil is soothing, calming and uplifting to the spirit. Also useful for stress, anxiety, depression, panic, trauma, hysteria, insomnia, sedative, nervous tension, bereavement, PMT and herpes.

Blends with: orange, lemon, geranium, rose geranium, chamomile, frankincense, lavender and ylang ylang.

Orange blossom

Neroli (Orange blossom) (T, M)

Citrus aurantium

Fragrance: exquisite, floral, sweet scent, both light and refreshing.

Known uses: toner, dry, mature skin, wrinkles, stretch marks, scar tissue, wounds, cuts, nervous indigestion, irritable bowel symptoms, relaxation, panic attacks, insomnia, vertigo, shock and sudden emotional upsets.

Blends with: citrus oils, clary sage, jasmine, lavender, geranium, lavender, sandalwood, rosemary and ylang ylang.

Melissa

Nutmeg (T, M)

Myristica fragrans

Fragrance: light, woody, warm-spicy aromatic.

Known uses: muscular and joint pains, rheumatism, arthritis, circulation, digestion, flatulence, diarrhoea, gallstones, mental fatigue, gout, supporting the reproductive system and stimulating the mind.

Blends with: cypress, black pepper, geranium, rosemary and clary sage.

Orange (Sweet) (T)

Citrus aurantium dulcis

Fragrance: sweet, fresh, fruity smell.

Known uses: digestion, constipation, tonic, digestion, liver, nervous indigestion, depression, tension headaches, cellulite, detoxing, obesity, constipation, influenza stress, colds and immune system.

Blends with: fennel, frankincense, black pepper, sandalwood, peppermint, ginger, vetiver and lavender.

Palmarosa (M)

Cymbopogon martini

Fragrance: soft, sweet, floral with gentle notes of lemon.

Known uses: An aromatic grass with a similar, but less expensive, fragrance to rose, therefore widely used in perfumery. Also useful for stress, anxiety, nervous tension, calming, uplifting, improving appetite, acne, diarrhoea eczema, urinary tract and skincare and as an antiseptic.

Blends with: bergamot, geranium, sandalwood, orange, lime, grapefruit, chamomile, rosemary and ylang ylang.

Nutmegs

Orange

Patchouli (B)

Pogostemon cablin

Fragrance: aromatic, woody and musky with spicy, musty, earthy-sweet undertones.

Known uses: depression, scars, acne, stretch marks, dry ageing skin, eczema, and as antiseptic and aphrodisiac.

Blends with: bergamot, clary sage, geranium, lavender, rose geranium, chamomile, cedarwood and myrrh.

Peppermint

Pine

Peppermint (T)

Mentha piperita

Fragrance: strong, fresh, minty aroma with sweet undertones.

Known uses: indigestion, stomach cramps, concentration, muscle pains, headaches and migraines, deodorant, nausea, coughs and colds.

Blends with: rosemary, black pepper, ginger, eucalyptus, lavender, marjoram, lemon and rosemary.

Pine (M)

Pinus sylvestris

Fragrance: fresh, forest smell with sweet balsamic tones.

Known uses: urinary infection, diuretic, tonic, colds, flu, bronchitis, rheumatism, cystitis, period pains, muscular aches and pains, deodorizing and antiseptic.

Blends with: cedarwood, cypress, lemon, eucalyptus, marjoram, juniper, lavender and rosemary.

Note: Rose essential oil has not been included in this section as it is now considered to be a skin sensitizer. Its use in commercial products is therefore heavily restricted to a maximum of 0.1% (0.1g per 100g of soap base = approx 1–2 drops). Instead of rose oil use a combination of rose geranium and palmarosa essential oils, or a rose fragrance oil.

Rose geranium

Petitgrain (T)

Citrus aurantium

Fragrance: fresh, green, floral smell with a hint of citrus and woody undertones.

Known uses: Petitgrain is distilled from the leaves and twigs of the bitter orange tree, whereas neroli is obtained from the orange flower of the same tree. Useful for stress, panic, nervous exhaustion, depression, muscle spasms, digestion, stomach cramps, insomnia, greasy skin, emotional conditions and as a general pick-me-up.

Blends with: juniper, clary sage, neroli, lavender, rosemary, bergamot, orange, jasmine, sandalwood, chamomile, lemon, palmarosa, geranium and ylang ylang.

Rosemary (T, M)

Rosmarinus officinalis

Fragrance: strong, fresh, herbaceous, camphoraceous scent.

Known uses: muscular aches and pains, rheumatism, painful periods, circulation, headaches, concentration, sprains, lymphatic drainage, digestion, colds and flu.

Blends with: cedarwood, geranium, bergamot, lavender, lemongrass and peppermint.

Rose geranium (T, M)

Pelargonium graveolens and *Pelargonium rosa*

Fragrance: fresh, crisp, sweet rosy scent.

Known uses: nervous system, PMT, anxiety, menopause, eczema, lymphatic system, jaundice, haemorrhoids, stress, gall stones, mild depression.

Blends with: bergamot, lime, lemon, cedarwood, clary sage, grapefruit, neroli, lavender, jasmine, rosemary and orange.

Rosemary

Sandalwood (B)

Santalum album

Fragrance: soft, deep, rich, sweet, exotic woody aroma.

Known uses: An oil widely used in the perfume and cosmetics industry. Useful for eczema, asthma, urinary and venereal infections, antiseptic, meditation, bronchitis, nervous exhaustion, chest infections, coughs and dry skin and as an aphrodisiac. Ensure that your sandalwood comes from a sustainable plantation and is ethically sourced.

Blends with: bergamot, palmarosa, geranium, vetiver, ylang ylang, jasmine, cedarwood, black pepper and myrrh.

Tangerine (T)

Citrus reticulata

Fragrance: fresh, sweet, orange-like citrus aroma.

Known uses: nervous system, stress, tension, calming, relaxing, constipation, digestive system, flatulence, diarrhoea, cellulite, stretch marks, circulation, fluid retention, stomach and liver problems and antiseptic.

Blends with: citrus oils, bergamot, cinnamon, frankincense, nutmeg, clary sage and lavender.

Tea tree

Tea tree (M)

Melaleuca alternifolia

Fragrance: strong, spicy, pungent camphoraceous smell.

Known uses: A native to Australia, tea tree has been used historically by the Aborigines as an antiseptic and for a variety of other medicinal purposes. Useful for the immune system, colds, influenza, antiviral, antibacterial, antifungal, muscle aches and pains, shock, skin infections, genital infections, cystitis, vaginal thrush, herpes, tuberculosis, bronchitis, asthma, coughs, sinusitis, oily skin, acne, abscesses, burns, athlete's foot, ringworm, cold sores, blemishes, warts, sunburn. *Caution: limit to 1%.*

Blends with: lavender, eucalyptus, rosemary, pine, lemon and thyme.

Thyme (M)

Thymus vulgaris

Fragrance: warm, sweet, spicy herbaceous scent.

Known uses: With its antibacterial, antifungal and antiviral properties, thyme was used throughout the ancient world for embalming and incense. It is useful for venereal infection, colds, flu, coughs, bronchitis, urinary infection, cystitis, respiratory infection, spasmodic coughs, asthma, digestive system, muscle stiffness, aches, pains, acne, rheumatism, arthritis, boils, lice and scabies.
Caution: Do not use if pregnant or if you have high blood pressure or on sensitive or damaged skin. Also, it should not be used in concentrations of more than 1%

Blends with: rosemary, geranium, bergamot, grapefruit, eucalyptus, lemon, lavender and pine.

Thyme

Vetiver (B)

Vetiveria zizanoides

Fragrance: Heavy, sweet, earthy, powerful, smoky scent with a woody, musty undertone.

Known uses: Vetiver is known as the 'oil of tranquillity' because of its deeply calming and relaxing properties. Useful for depression, arthritis, insomnia, stress, circulation, anaemia, muscular aches and pains, menstrual cramps, rheumatism, acne, wrinkles, stretch marks and mental and physical exhaustion.

Blends with: clary sage, lavender, jasmine, patchouli, sandalwood and ylang ylang.

Yarrow

Yarrow (T)

Achillea millefolium

Fragrance: penetrating green, sweet herbaceous aroma.

Known uses: Effective as a painkiller, antispasmodic and anti-inflammatory, for rheumatoid arthritis, skin disorders, sores, rashes, wounds, haemorrhoids, kidney, bladder, colon complaints, fatigue, insomnia, stress, circulation, muscular aches and pains. Yallow can be used in baby products at up to 0.5%.

Blends with: cedarwood, rosemary, chamomile, lavender, sandalwood, rose geranium, clary sage, lemon, grapefruit, peppermint, cypress, fennel, palmarosa, ylang ylang, frankincense, lemongrass, ginger, marjoram and vetiver.

Ylang ylang (T, M)

Cananga odorata

Fragrance: Intensely sweet, exotic, floral scent with a creamy top note.

Known uses: The name ylang ylang means 'flower of flowers'. There are different grades of this fragrant oil. The first distillation, ylang ylang extra, has the sweetest odour and is only used in the perfume industry. The oil used in aromatherapy is a blend of the other grades. Useful for stress, panic attacks, depression, anxiety, nervous conditions, aphrodisiac, high blood pressure, oily skin, hyperpnoea, rapid breathing and heartbeat, impotence and frigidity. *Caution: use in moderation (just one or two drops) as too much can bring on a headache or nausea.*

Blends with: sandalwood, jasmine, grapefruit, lavender, bergamot, rose geranium, cedarwood, jasmine, clary sage, lemon, vetiver and sandalwood.

Ylang ylang

Other ingredients

If you are using a colour, choose one that naturally complements and enhances your recipe. Blue is calming, red is stimulating, yellow is revitalizing, green is harmonizing and pink is tranquil.

Colours

Powdered herbs and spices can be used to add colour and texture to your products. Use annatto seeds for yellow, and alkanet root for a natural pink. However, natural ingredients often fade quickly, so do not leave your recipes in direct sunlight as the fragrance and colour may well be destroyed.

Cosmetic-grade liquid colour is the easiest cosmetic colour to use in soaps and bath bombs, although it is not suitable for oil-based recipes. Pigments such as ultramarines and oxides are powdered colours made up of several small particles: they are very strong and a tiny amount will go a long way, so beware. Use these sparingly in melts, bath bombs and opaque soaps. Mix them with a little water (or oil if adding to melts) first.

Note: Essential oils, fragrance and some additives may tint your product, so always make sure that you add the colouring last to get an accurate idea of the final colour.

Mica

Mica powders are very fine particles of naturally mined minerals from the rocks and the earth. They come in a huge range of wonderful colours and can add a beautiful pearlescence or iridescence to your oils and butters.

Mica

Alkanet root

Ultramarine pink powder colour

Recipes

Create your own spa with a refreshing bath oil to enliven your senses and soothe your skin. Ideal for restoring balance and vitality to help you cope with the coming week's stresses and strains.

Reviving bath oil

See pages 16–17 for basic oil recipe instructions.

What you will need

8¾oz (250ml) sweet almond oil

50 drops (2.5ml) lavender essential oil

25 drops (1.25ml) rosemary essential oil

20 drops (1ml) lime essential oil

5 drops petitgrain essential oil

Quantity

This recipe makes just over 8¾oz (250ml) of bath oil.

Instructions

Thoroughly mix all the ingredients in a jug and pour into a bottle. To use, pour 1–2 tablespoons (15–30ml) into a bath of warm running water.

This skin-quenching luxury butter is rich, creamy and smooth.
Use it on any part of your body that is in need of some tender loving
care, particularly hard-skin areas, such as feet, elbows or knees.

Butter me up

See pages 18–19 for basic body butter recipe instructions.

What you will need

4oz (120g) shea butter

2¾oz (80g) grapeseed oil

25 drops (1.25ml) lavender essential oil

½ teaspoon (2.5ml) vitamin E oil (optional)

Quantity

This recipe makes 7oz (200g) of body butter.

Instructions

Melt the shea butter in a double boiler. Remove from the heat and add the grapeseed, vitamin E and lavender oils. Place the pan in a bowl of iced water and whip by hand. When thick and creamy, spoon into containers and leave to set for 24 hours. To use, rub the butter between your palms; it will instantly melt. Apply to your skin, avoiding the area around your eyes.

Note *In warm weather store this butter in a refrigerator.*

Teenagers will love this deliciously moisturizing lip balm with all the benefits of punnets of strawberries packed into little jars. Take it on a picnic for the best-kept and delectable lips.

Sweet lips

See pages 24–25 for basic balm recipe instructions.

What you will need

2¾oz (80g) sweet almond oil
1oz (30g) beeswax (unrefined yellow with its natural honey scent is best)
1oz (30g) shea butter
½oz (15g) strawberry oil (optional – can be substituted with sweet almond oil)
Small pinch of alkanet root (optional)
½ teaspoon (2.5ml) vitamin E oil (optional)
20 drops (1ml) strawberry flavour oil

Quantity

This recipe makes three little jam pots of balm or nine small lip balms.

Instructions

Melt all the ingredients, except the strawberry flavour oil, in a double saucepan. When melted, strain the alkanet with a sieve and add the strawberry flavour oil. Pour into pots and leave to set for 24 hours. Apply to your lips using your fingertips.

Recreate the scent of an Italian spring morning, with the fragrance of mountain daffodils and orange blossoms after the rain with Eau de Cologne, designed in the eighteenth century by an Italian perfume maker.

Eau de cologne

See pages 33–37 for basic perfume recipe instructions.

What you will need

7oz (200ml) sweet almond oil

5¼oz (150ml) jojoba oil

90 drops (4.5ml) sweet orange essential oil

45 drops (2.25ml) lemon essential oil

40 drops (2ml) bergamot essential oil

9 drops petitgrain essential oil

9 drops neroli light (orange blossom) essential oil

8 drops lavender essential oil

6 drops rosemary essential oil

Quantity

This recipe makes 12½oz (360ml) of perfumed bath oil.

Instructions

Add the essential oils to the sweet almond and jojoba oil and stir thoroughly. Pour into bottles. To use, pour 1–2 tablespoons (15–30ml) into a warm bath.

Note *You can adapt this recipe by changing the amounts of oils.*

The combination of these highly enriching and moisturizing butters together with the nourishing fruit oil provides a wonderfully emollient butter – ideal for mature skin or for use after sunbathing.

Fruity whip

See pages 18–19 for basic butter recipe instructions.

What you will need

1oz (30g) shea butter
½oz (15g) avocado butter
½oz (15g) mango butter
1½oz (45g) peach or apricot oil (weighed)
½ teaspoon (2.5ml) vitamin E oil (optional)
20 drops (1ml) passionfruit fragrance oil (or essential oil)

Quantity

This recipe makes 3½oz (100g) of body butter.

Instructions

Melt the butters, then remove from heat and add the peach oil and fragrance (or essential oil). Place container in a bowl of iced water and whisk by hand. When thick and creamy, spoon the mixture into containers and leave to set for 24 hours. To use, rub the butter between the palms of your hands; it will instantly melt. Apply to areas of dry skin.

Note *Store in a cool dark place or in a refrigerator.*

Full of nuttiness and with a masculine blend of essential oils, this bath oil is the perfect gift for the man in your life. Macadamia nut oil is vitamin-rich and will keep skin hydrated and supple.

Let's go nuts

See pages 16–17 for basic oil recipe instructions.

What you will need

7oz (200ml) sweet almond oil

1¾oz (50ml) macadamia nut oil

75 drops (3.75ml) tangerine essential oil
(or mandarin or sweet orange essential oil)

30 drops (1.5ml) cedarwood essential oil

45 drops (2.25ml) bay essential oil

Quantity

This recipe makes 9oz (255ml) of bath oil.

Instructions

Combine all the ingredients in a jug and mix thoroughly. Pour into a bottle. To use, pour 1–2 tablespoons (15–30ml) into a warm running bath.

Pretty in pink, these gorgeous little bath melts are a great moisturizing treat. With a sensual blend of essential oils they will leave your skin feeling silky-smooth and soft. They also make great little party favours.

Pretty tarts

See pages 26–27 for basic bath melts recipe instructions.

What you will need

7oz (200g) cocoa butter (use unrefined for the natural aroma)
3½oz (100g) sweet almond oil (weighed)
100 drops (5ml) rose geranium essential oil
50 drops (2.5ml) sandalwood essential oil
25 drops (1.25ml) ylang ylang essential oil
½ teaspoon ultramarine pink powder
½ teaspoon (2.5ml) vitamin E oil (optional)
18 pink rose buds

Quantity

This recipe makes approximately 18 small tarts.

Instructions

Mix a little pink colour with some sweet almond oil. Melt the cocoa butter in a double boiler, then add the remaining almond oil and mixed colour. Remove from heat and add the essential oils. Place a rose bud in each mould (mini silicone petit four moulds or ice cube moulds) and pour the mixture on top. Leave to set overnight. To use, simply pop into the bath.

Reduce the appearance of cellulite while toning your muscles and improving your skin's texture with firming juniper and grapefruit oils. Simply massage the firming body oil into any problem areas after exfoliating.

Firming body oil

See pages 16–19 for basic oil recipe instructions.

What you will need

5¼oz (150ml) sweet almond oil (or peach oil)
1¾oz (50ml) jojoba oil
30 drops (1.5ml) grapefruit essential oil
10 drops juniper essential oil

Quantity

This recipe will make just over 7oz (200ml) of body oil.

Instructions

Combine all the ingredients in a jug and mix thoroughly. Pour into a bottle. To use, pour some oil into the palms of your hands and massage into your hips, thighs and legs. Or draw a warm bath and add 1–2 tablespoons (15–30ml) of the oil to the bath water. Mix well to make sure that the oil has evenly dispersed, then simply lie back and relax.

Have fun trawling through flea markets for pretty little pill boxes, snuff boxes or antique make-up compacts to use as lip balm containers. These lip balms make lovely little retro presents to give to all your friends.

Get lippy

See pages 24–25 for basic balm recipe instructions.

What you will need

1oz (30g) olive oil (weighed)

⅓oz (10g) beeswax

⅓oz (10g) shea butter

½ teaspoon (2.5ml) vitamin E oil (optional)

Pinch of alkanet root (optional – this provides the natural pink/red colour)

Quantity

This recipe makes approximately four lip balms.

Instructions

Melt all the ingredients in a double saucepan. When melted, strain the alkanet with a sieve, pour into containers and leave to set for 24 hours. Apply to your lips with your fingertips.

Note *I prefer to use unrefined yellow beeswax for its lovely honey scent; use white beeswax pellets if you wish to keep your lip balm unscented. To add further fragrance, use 5 drops of cosmetic-safe flavour oil.*

This vitamin-rich face oil will rejuvenate tired skin and help to reduce the appearance of fine lines. Massage the oil into your face in an upward motion to help lymphatic drainage and leave the skin plump and firm.

Face up to it

See pages 16–17 for basic oil recipe instructions.

What you will need

1¾oz (50ml) sweet almond oil
¾oz (20ml) rose hip oil
¾oz (20ml) passionflower oil
⅓oz (10ml) raspberry oil
8 drops lavender essential oil
8 drops rose geranium essential oil
4 drops neroli light (orange blossom) essential oil
(If you are unable to obtain passionflower or raspberry oil substitute with jojoba or evening primrose oil.)

Quantity

This recipe will make approximately 3½oz (100ml) of face oil.

Instructions

Combine all the ingredients in a jug and mix thoroughly. Pour into bottles. To use, dab a small amount of oil into your palms and rub together. Gently pat your hands over your face and your neck.

Show the one you love that you care by creating a wonderful massage oil to arouse the senses. Alternatively, pour some oil into warm running water for a candlelit bath *à deux*.

Love potion

See pages 16–17 for basic oil recipe instructions.

What you will need

10½oz (300ml) sweet almond oil
10 drops sandalwood essential oil
10 drops patchouli essential oil
4 drops ylang ylang essential oil
2 drops clary sage essential oil

Quantity

This recipe will make approximately 10½oz (300ml) of oil.

Instructions

Thoroughly blend all the ingredients, then pour into a bottle. Pour some oil into the palms of your hands and massage into your skin in slow rhythmic movements. Or run a warm bath and add 1–2 tablespoons (15–30ml) of the oil to the water. Mix well to ensure that all the oil has evenly dispersed, then enjoy a leisurely soak.

Rise and shine with a smile with this invigorating oil.
The zesty lemongrass, zingy peppermint and energy-boosting
cypress will give you an extra early-morning lift.

Stimulating body oil

See pages 16–17 for basic oil recipe instructions.

What you will need

3½oz (100ml) sweet almond oil
16 drops cypress essential oil
14 drops lemongrass essential oil
10 drops peppermint essential oil

Quantity

This recipe will make approximately 3½oz (100ml) of oil.

Instructions

Combine all the ingredients in a jug and mix thoroughly.
Pour into a bottle. To use, pour some oil into the palms of
your hands and massage into your skin. Or run a warm bath
and add 1–2 tablespoons (15–30ml) of the oil to the water.
Mix well to ensure that all the oil has evenly dispersed, climb
in and relax.

Take a soak in this wonderfully indulgent, milky bath oil and give yourself some precious moments of peace and tranquillity. The exquisitely sensual scents will lift your spirits, calm your nerves and nourish your skin.

Decadent bath milk

See pages 16–17 for basic oil recipe instructions.

What you will need

6oz (170ml) unscented liquid soap base (SLS-free)

2¾oz (80ml) sweet almond oil

50 drops (2.5ml) jasmine absolute (or lavender essential oil)

50 drops (2.5ml) neroli light essential oil (or petitgrain)

50 drops (2.5ml) rose geranium essential oil

Quantity

This recipe makes approximately 8¾oz (250ml) of bath milk.

Instructions

Combine all the ingredients and mix thoroughly, then pour into a bottle. This mixture will settle and separate, so give it a good shake before pouring 1–2 tablespoons (15–30ml) into a bath of warm running water.

Note *You can reduce the cost by using other essential oils of your choice. I would also recommend using a SLS-free product that will not foam and dry your skin, but instead leave it as soft as silk.*

Bath bombs are a fun way to introduce moisturizing oils into your bath. As they fizz and bob around in the water they release their wonderful scent and any rose buds or petals enclosed within them.

Rosey cheeks

See pages 16–17 for basic oil recipe instructions.

What you will need

10½oz (300g) granulated citric acid
21oz (600g) bicarbonate of soda (baking soda)
75 drops (3.75ml) rose geranium essential oil
25 drops (1.25ml) patchouli essential oil
1 tablespoon (15ml) rose hip oil
A few rose buds or petals

Quantity

This recipe makes approximately three bath bombs.

Instructions

Place the citric acid in a bowl and sieve the bicarbonate on top. Add the essential oils and rose hip oil, then mix it with your hands. Wet your hands and shake some water into the mix – just enough to make it feel like damp sand. Place a rose bud in the bottom of each mould and press the mixture on top. Turn out onto a baking sheet and leave to set for 24 hours.

This deliciously chocolate-orange lip balm is made with real chocolate and will leave your lips effortlessly kissable. I defy anyone not to lick their super-smooth lips once they don this mouth-watering lip balm.

Chocolate kisses

See pages 24–25 for basic balm recipe instructions.

What you will need

1½oz (45g) hempseed oil (weighed)

1oz (30g) dark chocolate orange (or 70% chocolate)

½oz (15g) organic unrefined cocoa butter

½oz (15g) beeswax (unrefined yellow is best)

½ teaspoon (2.5ml) vitamin E oil (optional)

Quantity

This recipe makes approximately three lip balms.

Instructions

Melt all the ingredients in a double saucepan. Pour into empty clean mini-pâté jars or little pots and leave to set for 24 hours. Apply to your lips with your fingertips.

Note *If you wish to fragrance your lip balm, use 10 drops of cosmetic-safe flavour oil.*

Throughout history, the essential oils in this blend, together with the olive oil, have been used to rub into aching joints or muscles to ease discomfort and to soothe the skin.

Feeling peachy

See pages 16–17 for basic oil recipe instructions.

What you will need

5¼oz (150ml) peach oil (or apricot or sweet almond oil)

5¼oz (150ml) olive oil

24 drops (1.25ml) eucalyptus essential oil

12 drops cajeput essential oil

12 drops black pepper essential oil

12 drops ginger essential oil

Quantity

This recipe will make approximately 10½oz (300ml) of oil.

Instructions

Combine all the ingredients and mix thoroughly, then pour into a bottle. To use, pour some oil into the palms of your hands and rub into sore joints or muscles. Or draw a warm bath and add 1–2 tablespoons (15–30ml) of the oil to the water. Mix well to make sure that all the oil has evenly dispersed, climb into the bath and relax.

These fabulous moisturizing truffles make great party favours. Roll them in herbs, petals, cocoa powder or chocolate sprinkles to delight your guests. Just remember to label them 'not to eat' as they look yummy and smell divine.

Party truffles

See pages 28–29 for basic bath truffle recipe instructions.

What you will need
4½oz (125g) bicarbonate of soda (baking soda)
1¾oz (50g) citric acid
1oz (30g) cornflour (cornstarch)
1¾oz (50g) cocoa butter (use unrefined for a natural aroma)
50 drops (2.5ml) sweet orange essential oil
½ teaspoon (2.5ml) rose geranium essential oil
½ teaspoon (2.5ml) patchouli essential oil
½ teaspoon (2.5ml) vitamin E oil (optional)
1 packet of sprinkles and a handful of marigold petals

Quantity
This recipe makes approximately eight or nine mini-truffles.

Instructions
Melt the cocoa butter and vitamin E. Leave to cool slightly (although it should still be runny), and add the essential oils. Sieve the bicarbonate and cornflour, then add the citric acid. Add this mixture to the dry ingredients and stir until the consistency resembles moulding clay. Quickly shape into balls and roll in the sprinkles or petals. Leave to set for 24 hours.

Massage this soothing oil into your little ones' skin, to help them relax and drift off to sleep. This is a great natural alternative to products containing petrochemicals, giving your baby a healthier start in life.

Baby oil

See pages 16–17 for basic oil recipe instructions.

What you will need

10½oz (300ml) sweet almond oil (or olive oil)

10 drops lavender essential oil

10 drops rose geranium essential oil

5 drops chamomile essential oil

(The oils above can be substituted with mandarin or yarrow essential oils).

Quantity

This recipe makes 10½oz (300ml) of baby oil.

Instructions

Combine all the ingredients and mix thoroughly, then pour into a bottle. To use, pour a little oil into your palms, then massage into your baby's skin. Or draw a warm bath and add 1 tablespoon (15ml) of the oil to the water. Mix well to ensure that the oil has evenly dispersed.

Note *This recipe can be used on babies two weeks old and upwards. Do not exceed the amounts of essential oils stated. The oil will make the bath slippy, so make sure that you keep a firm hold of baby.*

This ultra-soft balm is great for soothing cradle cap and nappy rash or for people with sensitive skin, eczema or psoriasis. Either leave it unscented for the ultra sensitive, or add soothing lavender and calming mandarin oils.

Baby balm

See pages 24–25 for basic balm recipe instructions.

What you will need

2¾oz (80g) sweet almond oil (weighed)
⅓oz (10g) beeswax
½oz (15g) shea butter
⅓oz (10g) calendula oil (weighed)
¼ teaspoon (1.25ml) vitamin E oil (optional)
5 drops lavender essential oil (optional)
5 drops mandarin essential oil (optional)

Quantity

This recipe makes approximately one medium-sized balm 3½oz (100ml) and one travel-sized balm ¾oz (20ml).

Instructions

Melt all the ingredients in a double saucepan. Remove from the heat and add the essential oils, if using. Pour into containers and leave to set for 24 hours. Store in small, clean jam jars or in small aluminium tins.

Hair dyes, styling products and sodium lauryl sulphate (SLS) can strip your hair of its natural oils and irritate your scalp. This hair and scalp oil will restore nourishment, leaving your crowning glory in tip-top condition.

Top condition

See pages 16–17 for basic oil recipe instructions.

What you will need

3½oz (100ml) olive oil

2½oz (75ml) avocado oil

2oz (60ml) jojoba oil

½ teaspoon (2.5ml) neem oil

30 drops (1.5ml) lavender essential oil

20 drops (1ml) rosemary essential oil

20 drops (1ml) patchouli essential oil

10 drops tea tree essential oil

Quantity

This recipe makes 8½oz (240ml) of hair conditioning oil.

Instructions

Combine all the ingredients and mix thoroughly. Pour into bottles. To use, pour 1–2 tablespoons (15–30ml) into the palms of your hands and massage into your hair and scalp. Leave for five minutes before washing off with shampoo.

Note *Your scalp will benefit from an organic SLS-free shampoo.*

Why not try making your own moisturizing organic soap?
It's simple to make, inexpensive, and contains readily available
materials, while leaving you and your baby's skin wonderfully soft.

Soothing soap

See pages 20–23 for basic soap recipe instructions.

What you will need

35oz (1kg) vegetable glycerine soap base
(organic, natural or SLS-free)
1 tablespoon (15ml) calendula petals or other herbs
(Do not use lavender or rose petals as these will go brown)
1 tablespoon (15ml) calendula oil
30 drops (1.5ml) lavender essential oil
30 drops (1.5ml) chamomile essential oil
30 drops (1.5ml) mandarin essential oil

Quantity

This recipe will make approximately seven regular-sized bars.

Instructions

Melt the soap base in a saucepan until liquid. Remove from
the heat and add the calendula oil, petals and essential oils.
Pour into a plastic container and leave to set overnight.
Cut slices of the soap with a kitchen knife.

Note *For people over seven, increase the essential oils to 1tsp (5ml).*

A valuable balm for those little emergencies, such as bruises, scrapes, burns, insect bites and inflammations. The healing and antibacterial properties of lavender are legendary and have been utilized throughout history.

First-aid balm

See pages 24–25 for basic balm recipe instructions.

What you will need

2oz (60g) olive oil (weighed)

1oz (30g) beeswax

1oz (30g) shea butter

⅓oz (10g) comfrey oil (weighed)

⅓oz (10g) St John's Wort (weighed)

⅓oz (10g) calendula oil (weighed)

½ teaspoon (2.5ml) vitamin E oil (optional)

20 drops (1ml) lavender essential oil

10 drops manuka (or tea tree) essential oil

Quantity

This recipe will make three regular-sized and three mini balms.

Instructions

Melt all the ingredients except the essential oils in a double saucepan. Remove from the heat and add the essential oils. Pour into containers and leave to set for 24 hours.

Note *Arnica could be substituted for St John's Wort, but should not be applied to broken skin.*

Made from lashings of cocoa butter and dark chocolate, these gorgeous bath treats look and smell good enough to eat. Although tantalizing, keep them away from the taste buds and pop them straight in the tub.

Chocolate melts

See pages 26–27 for basic bath melt instructions.

What you will need

3½oz (100g) organic unrefined cocoa butter
1¾oz (50g) sweet almond oil (weighed)
¾oz (25g) dark chocolate
1 teaspoon (5ml) chocolate truffle or black cafe fragrance oil (optional)

Quantity

This recipe makes approximately 6oz (170g) of mixture. The number of melts will depend on the size of the moulds.

Instructions

Melt the cocoa butter, remove from the heat and add the sweet almond oil and fragrance oil, if using. Pour the mixture into the chocolate (or ice cube) moulds and leave to set overnight, ideally in a refrigerator. To use, simply pop a melt into a warm bath.

Note *These will melt in a warm environment, so keep them in a refrigerator. The melts look and smell tasty but are inedible and should be kept out of the reach of children and pets.*

A sumptuous shimmering body butter to make you feel just like a movie screen goddess. Envelop your body in this glowing silky butter and allow the studio lights to make your skin shine.

Goddess body glow

See pages 18–19 for basic butter instructions.

What you will need

1½oz (45g) shea butter

1oz (30g) jojoba oil

½ teaspoon (2.5ml) vitamin E oil (optional)

5 drops petitgrain essential oil

3 drops lavender essential oil

2 drops frankincense essential oil

½–1 teaspoon cosmetic-grade gold mica

Quantity

This recipe makes 2½oz (75g) of body butter.

Instructions

Melt the shea butter and vitamin E oil. Remove from the heat and add the jojoba and essential oils. Place pan in a bowl of iced water and whip with a hand whisk. When it thickens, add the gold mica. Keep whipping until thick and creamy, then spoon into containers. Leave to set for 24 hours. To use, rub between your palms and apply from the neck downwards.

Storage

Store in a cool, dark place or a refrigerator to prevent it melting.

This soothing salve protects and nourishes hard-working hands. Carrot tissue oil smoothes dry chapped skin, borage repairs the skin, wheatgerm reduces scar tissue, and comfrey soothes bruises – all in one very handy balm!

Very handy

See pages 24–25 for basic balm instructions.

What you will need

2oz (60g) olive oil (weighed)
⅝oz (20g) beeswax
½oz (15g) shea butter
1oz (30g) wheatgerm oil (weighed)
⅓oz (10g) comfrey oil (weighed)
⅓oz (10g) borage (starflower) oil (weighed)
⅓oz (10g) carrot tissue oil (weighed)
½ teaspoon (2.5ml) vitamin E oil (optional)
12 drops rose geranium essential oil
10 drops frankincense essential oil
8 drops lemon essential oil

Quantity

This recipe makes approximately 5½oz (160ml) of hand salve.

Instructions

Melt the beeswax, shea butter, olive oil and vitamin E in a double boiler. Remove from the heat and add the remaining ingredients. Stir thoroughly, pour into pots and leave for 24 hours.

Aloe has been used for centuries for relieving burns, acne and cuts, as well as for easing allergic reactions and insect bites. This butter will instantly melt on contact with your skin, leaving it soothed and supple.

Burnt out

See pages 18–19 for basic butter instructions.

What you will need

1⅓oz (40g) jojoba oil (weighed)
⅝oz (20g) cocoa butter
⅝oz (20g) aloe butter
⅝oz (20g) mango butter
¼ teaspoon (1.25ml) vitamin E oil (optional)
12 drops lavender essential oil
12 drops chamomile essential oil

Quantity

This recipe will make 3½oz (100g) body butter.

Instructions

Melt the butters and vitamin E. Remove from the heat and add the jojoba and essential oils. Place the pan in a bowl of iced water and whip the mixture with a hand whisk. When it is thick and creamy, spoon the mixture into containers and leave to set for 24 hours. To use, rub the butter between the palms of your hands and gently massage into afflicted areas.

Storage

When hot, store the butter in the refrigerator to prevent it melting.

After a long cold walk, run yourself a steaming hot bath. Add some of this spicy oil and let the essential oils of ginger, pepper, orange and cinnamon stimulate your circulation and warm up your body.

Hot stuff

See pages 16–17 for basic bath oil instructions.

What you will need

10½oz (300ml) grapeseed oil
100 drops (5ml) sweet orange essential oil
30 drops (1.5ml) black pepper essential oil
30 drops (1.5ml) ginger essential oil
10 drops cinnamon essential oil

Quantity

This recipe makes approximately 10½oz (300ml) of bath oil.

Instructions

Combine all the ingredients and mix thoroughly. Pour in a bottle. To use, pour 1–2 tablespoons (15–30ml) of oil into a bath of hot running water.

When on the go, carry a small lotion bar with you and whenever your skin needs refreshing or a boost of moisture simply rub the bar onto the affected areas for quick, convenient relief for dry skin.

Solid lotion bar

What you will need

3oz (90g) beeswax

3oz (90g) olive oil (weighed)

3oz (90g) shea butter

1 teaspoon (5ml) vitamin E oil (optional)

15 drops lemon essential oil (or lemongrass)

15 drops lavender essential oil

15 drops mandarin essential oil

8 drops frankincense essential oil

Quantity

This recipe makes approximately three or four lotion bars.

Instructions

Melt all the ingredients, except the essential oils. Remove from heat and add the essential oils. Pour into moulds and leave to set for 24 hours. To use, simply rub the bar over areas of dry skin.

Note *These melt in the heat, so leave at home in hot weather.*

Look after your feet and they will look after you! Soak them in a basin of warm water and epsom salts, then treat them to this comforting foot balm containing aromatic Moroccan argan oil and moisturizing shea butter.

Completely balmy

See pages 24–25 for basic balm instructions.

What you will need

1oz (30g) olive oil

½oz (15g) beeswax

½oz (15g) shea butter

½oz (15g) argan oil (weighed)

½ teaspoon (2.5ml) vitamin E oil (optional)

5 drops lemongrass essential oil

5 drops eucalyptus essential oil

5 drops tea tree essential oil (or manuka)

Quantity

This recipe makes two medium-sized balms.

Instructions

Melt all of the ingredients except the essential oils. Remove from the heat and add the essential oils. Pour into containers and leave to set for 24 hours. Rub between your hands and apply to clean exfoliated feet.

To wind down at the end of a long day, run a warm bath and pour in some soothing, aromatic bath oil, light a candle and relax in the fragrant aroma. A ritual practised by ancient civilisations since time immemorial.

That's oil folks!

See pages 16–17 for basic oil instructions.

What you will need
3½oz (100ml) sweet almond oil
3½oz (100ml) jojoba oil
25 drops (1.25ml) lavender essential oil
12 drops frankincense essential oil
12 drops petitgrain essential oil

Quantity
This recipe will make just over 7oz (200ml) of bath oil.

Instructions
Mix the ingredients together and pour into your container.
To use, pour 1–2 tablespoons (15–30ml) into a bath of warm running water.

Conversions

The table below is a general guide for the measurements throughout the book. Please note that the imperial measurements are approximate conversions from metric.

When following the instructions, use either the metric or the imperial measurements, do not mix units. For practical reasons, measurements below 1ml have been left as drops only.

Volume

20 drops = 1ml	1 teaspoon = 5ml	1oz = 30ml
40 drops = 2ml	2 teaspoon = 10ml	2oz = 60ml
60 drops = 3ml	1 tablespoon = 15ml	3oz = 85ml
80 drops = 4ml	2 tablespoons = 30ml	4oz = 120ml
100 drops = 5ml		5oz = 140ml

Dry weights

1oz = 30g

2oz = 60g

3oz = 90g

4oz = 120g

5oz = 140g

Suppliers

Many pharmacies and health food shops will supply essential oils, herbs and carrier oils for cosmetic use. However you will need to purchase butters, cosmetic colour, fragrance and soap base from a supplier of cosmetic ingredients.

The following are a list of mail order/internet-based companies; the addresses provided are their trading addresses, which are warehouses and are not open to the public unless specified.

UK

Amphora Aromatics
www.amphora-aromatics.com
Cotham, Bristol
Tel: +44 (0) 117 904 7212
Wide range of essential oils, oils and aromatherapy supplies, carrier oils.

Aromantic Ltd
www.aromantic.co.uk
Forres, Moray
Tel: +44 (0) 1309 696900
Good range of cosmetic ingredients, oils, butters, soap bases etc.

Cakes Cookies & Crafts Shop
www.cakescookiesandcraftsshop.co.uk
Morecambe, Lancashire
Tel: +44 (0) 1524 389684
Huge range of fun chocolate moulds and chocolate supplies.

E H Thorne (Beehives) Ltd
www.thorne.co.uk
Redhill, Surrey
Tel: +44 (0) 1673 858555
Shop and website for beekeepers. Huge range of beeswax and melters.

G. Baldwin & Co
www.baldwins.co.uk
London
Tel: +44 (0) 20 7703 5550
Herb specialists – vast range of herbs, essential oils, carrier oils, macerated oils, wax, flower essences and a shop.

Gracefruit
www.gracefruit.com
Longcroft, Stirlingshire
Tel: +44 (0)141 416 2906
A wide range of ingredients, plus unusual and interesting butters, fragrances and oils. Large range of vegetable waxes.

Just a Soap
www.justasoap.co.uk
Whepstead, Bury St Edmunds
Tel: +44 (0) 1284 735043
All soap-making ingredients, moulds, bath-bomb and soap ingredients, oils, butters and containers.

New Directions (UK)
www.newdirectionsuk.com
Fordingbridge, Hampshire,
Tel: +44 (0) 1425 655555
Huge range of ingredients including most butters, oils, essential oils, soap bases; wide range of bottles, jars and containers.

Sheabutter Cottage
www.sheabuttercottage.co.uk
Sonning, Reading
Tel: +44 (0) 118 9693830
Exotic and fair trade oils, butters, essential oils and other ingredients.

Soap Basics
www.soapbasics.co.uk
Melksham, Wiltshire
Tel: +44 (0) 1225 899286
E-mail: info@soapbasics.co.uk
A good range of ingredients, fragrances, herbs, oils and butters, bath bomb and soap-making ingredients. A wide selection of different-coloured micas.

The British Wax Refining Co. Ltd
www.britishwax.com
Redhill, Surrey
Tel: +44 (0) 1737 761242
Email: wax@britishwax.com
Suppliers of wax.

The Soap Kitchen
www.thesoapkitchen.co.uk
Torrington, Devon
Tel: +44 (0) 1805 622944
Email: info@thesoapkitchen.co.uk
All the ingredients you need to make the recipes in this book. A huge range of ingredients, soap (and liquid soap) bases, bath-bomb ingredients, moulds, butters, colour, herbs, oils, containers and bottles. Large range of fragrances.

The Soapmakers Store
www.soapmakers-store.com
Horsham, West Sussex
Tel: +44 (0) 844 800 3386
All soap-making ingredients, oils, butters, essential oils etc.

USA & Canada

Bramble Berry Inc.
www.brambleberry.com
Bellingham, WA 98225
Tel: 360/734-8278,
Toll Free: 877-627-7883
Huge range of ingredients, oils, butters, soap (and liquid soap) bases, and bath bomb making ingredients, fragrances, oils and moulds.

Camden-Grey Essential Oils Inc.
www.camdengrey.com
Doral, FL 33122
Toll-free line for orders only:
866-503-8615
Tel: 305-500-9630
Email: orderdesk@camdengrey.com
Wide range of essential oils, absolutes, oils, butters, soap base and moulds.

Cranberry Lane
www.cranberrylane.com
Richmond, BC V6X 2T1
Toll-Free: 1-800-833-4533
Local: 604-944-1488
Good supply of most ingredients.

Custom Chocolate Shop
www.customchocolateshop.com
Canadensis, PA 18325
Tel: 570-595-2880
Email: kristin@customchocolateshop.com
Large range of chocolate, moulds including personalized moulds, boxes, ties, wrappers.

From Nature With Love
www.fromnaturewithlove.com
Oxford, CT 06478
Tel: (800) 520-2060 or (203) 267-6061
Extensive range of ingredients; huge range of butters, soap bases, ingredients and moulds.

Herbal Accents
www.herbalaccents.com
Alpinie, CA 91903-0937
Tel: 619-562-2650
Email: sales@herbalaccents.com
Good range of ingredients and moulds.

Kangaroo Blue
www.kangarooblue.com
Plainfield, IL 60585
Store: 815-609-9275
Phone: 815-609-9275
Oils, butters, waxes, soap bases and essential oils.

Mountain Rose Herbs

www.mountainroseherbs.com

Eugene, OR 97405

Voice (800) 879-3337

International Calls (541) 741-7307

Certified organic herb specialists; good range of oils butters, essential oils and bottles.

Majestic Mountain Sage

www.thesage.com

Logan, Utah 84321

Tel: 435-755-0863

Oils, butters, soap bases and all other cosmetic ingredients and moulds.

Milky Way Molds

www.milkywaymolds.com

Portland, OR 97206

Tel: 503-774-4157

Email: contact@milkywaymolds.com

Designers and manufacturers of a huge range of unique, fun moulds.

New Directions Aromatics (USA)

www.newdirectionsaromatics.com

San Ramon, CA 94583

Tel: 1-800-246-7817 (Toll-free)

Email: sales@newdirectionsaromatics.com

Huge range of ingredients including most butters, oils, essential oils, soap bases; excellent range of bottles and jars.

New Directions Aromatics (Canada)

www.newdirectionsaromatics.ca

Ontario L7A 1C5 Canada

Tel: 905-840-5459

Order Desk: 1-877-255-7692 (Toll-free)

Email: oils@newdirectionsaromatics.ca

Huge range of ingredients including most butters, oils, essential oils, soap bases; excellent range of bottles and jars.

The Chemistry Store

www.chemistrystore.com

Cayce, SC 29033

Toll-free: 800-224-1430

Email: sales@chemistrystore.com

Order Inquires: glitter@chemistrystore.com

All soap-making ingredients; good range of butters, oils, balm moulds, containers.

The Essential Oil Company

www.essentialoil.com

Oregon 97202

Toll-free: 800-729-5912

Tel (local): 503-872-8735

- Oregon 503-872-8772

Organic, wildcrafted and cultivated essential oils, molds, oils, soap bases.

The Scent Works

www.store.scent-works.com

North Carolina

27702-0828

Tel: 1-973-598-9600

Email: Sales:TheScentworks.com

Oils, butters, fragrance and essential oils, herbs, containers.

Snowdrift Farm, Inc.

www.snowdriftfarm.com

Tucson, AZ 85713 USA

Tel: 520-882-7080

Toll-free: 888-999-6950

Wide range of all ingredients.

Australia and New Zealand

AquaSapone
www.aquasapone.com.au
NSW 2304, Australia
(From Australia 00151 781 9988427)
Oils, butters and essential oils.

Aussie Soap Supplies
www.aussiesoapsupplies.com.au
Palmyra WA 6957
(Visits to workshop by appointment)
Tel: (08) 9339 1885
Email: david@aussiesoapsupplies.com.au
*Oils, butters, soap bases, cosmetic
ingredients.*

Big Tree Supplies
www.big-tree.com.au
Alderley QLD 4051
Tel +61 (0)7 33524395
Email: info@big-tree.com.au
*Loads of moulds for melts, soaps and
bath bombs. Fragrance and flavour oils.*

Essential Oils and Soap
www.oilsandsoap.com.au
Beaconsfield TAS 7270
Tel: (03) 6394 3737
Email: info@oilsandsoap.com.au
*Oils, butters, lip balm flavours, moulds and
soap bases.*

Heirloom Body Care
www.heirloombodycare.com.au
Llandilo NSW 2747
(Visitors by appointment)
Tel: (02) 4777 4457
Email: heirloom@heirloombodycare.
com.au
*Oils, butters, huge range of lip-balm
packaging and accessories including
lip-balm flavours and ingredients, lovely
lip-balm tins, good range of cosmetic
packaging, soap bases, liquid soap bases,
and many other supplies.*

New Directions
www.newdirections.com.au
Sydney, NSW 2204
Tel: 61 2 8577 5999
Toll-free: 1800 637 697
Email: nda@newdirections.com.au
*Huge range of ingredients including most
butters, oils, essential oils, soap bases,
excellent range of bottles and jars.*

Manuka Oil.com
www.manukaoil.com
Bio-Extracts Limited.
South Auckland, New Zealand.
Phone: +64 9 236 0917
Email: email@ManukaOil.com
Manuka essential oil.

About the author

Elaine Stavert formed The Littlecote Soap Co. after a life-changing move from her television career in London to a farm in the beautiful Buckinghamshire countryside. Surrounded by hedgerows and meadows, and with a keen interest in herbalism and aromatherapy, Elaine was soon developing a range of natural toiletries, bath products and candles that were eco-friendly, kind to the skin and quintessentially English. Elaine's passion for her products is evident in the pure and natural ingredients that she uses in imaginative ways to produce traditional recipes with contemporary twists.

The Littlecote Soap Co.
Littlecote Farm
Littlecote
Nr Dunton
Buckingham
MK18 3LN
www.littlecotesoap.co.uk

Acknowledgements

Robert, Diane and Pearl
For love, encouragement, patience and support.

I would also like to thank my wonderful team at The Littlecote Soap Co.: Caroline Heron, Nikki Jellis, Rebecca Gulliver, Andrea Ellis, Alison Vinter, Carole Capel, Jess Bliss, Diane Winks and my Business Partner Pearl Olney, for their hard work, dedication and patience while I have been writing this book. My thanks also to all those at Littlecote Farm, Sean Jackman and Mr Nab for their sense of humour and for introducing me to a whole new array of natural aromas. To beekeepers Jonathan and Rebecca Longley for taking me beekeeping and making sure that I was not stung. Rob Case-Green from British Wax. And finally to Benjamin Hedges from J. Hedges and Sons for reminding us of traditional values and without whom the company would not exist.

My thanks also to the talented team at GMC Publishing, to Jonathan Bailey and Gerrie Purcell for inviting me to write this book, to Beth Wicks for her editing skills, professionalism and patience, and to Rob Janes and Gilda Pacitti for their creative eye for detail and design.

Photography acknowledgements

Main project photography by Laurel Guilfoyle.
Step-by-step photography by Elaine Stavert.
All other photography by Anthony Bailey except Dennis Wong/Flickr (page 11) and Michael Bevens (page 73).

Index

Names of recipes are given in italics

To place an order, or to request a catalogue, contact:

GMC Publications Ltd

Castle Place, 166 High Street, Lewes, East Sussex, BN7 1XU

Tel: +44 (0)1273 488005 **Website:** www.gmcbooks.com

Orders by credit card are accepted